GLOUCESTERSHIRE

Extracted from

AN INVENTORY OF NONCONFORMIST CHAPELS AND MEETING-HOUSES IN CENTRAL ENGLAND

PREFACE

Nonconformist places of worship have for some years been the subject of detailed investigation by the Royal Commission on the Historical Monuments of England, and the records accumulated, nation-wide, will be available in the archives of the National Monuments Record. The following pages form part of the first published volume resulting from these investigations, *An Inventory of Nonconformist Chapels and Meeting-houses in Central England* (HMSO 1986). This is, however, a substantial volume, and for reasons of convenience and local interest it has also been divided into county fascicules for individual publication and separate sale, the pagination of the full *Inventory* being retained.

The subject is taken to include not only the Old Dissent of Presbyterians, Independents, Baptists and Quakers but also the New Dissent of the 18th century, the Methodists and Moravians, together with denominations of more recent origin.

Over the years denominational names have been subject to alteration: some by re-grouping, notably with the formation in 1972 of the United Reformed Church (URC); others by the more gradual process of reunion and doctrinal evolution. Original doctrinal names have, where possible, been used throughout, subsequent changes being noted in the text except in the case of Methodist groups of which only a few remained independent after 1932.

The work of investigation and recording of nonconformist places of worship, for archive and publication, has been entirely the responsibility of Mr Christopher Stell of the Commission staff. Much of it was completed before the changes in local government boundaries of 1974, and in *Inventory* and fascicules the county names and boundaries obtaining immediately prior to that date have been retained.

ABBREVIATIONS

NMR   National Monuments Record
RCHM   Royal Commission on the Historical Monuments of England
URC   United Reformed Church

BIBLIOGRAPHICAL SOURCES
other than those fully titled in the text

GLOUCESTERSHIRE

Arnold, H. Godwin 1960	'Early Meeting Houses', *Trans. Anc. Monum. Soc.*, NS VIII (1960) 89–139.
Belden, A. D. *c.* 1930	*George Whitefield – The Awakener* [*c.* 1930].
Blake, S. T. 1979	*Cheltenham's Churches and Chapels AD 773–1883.*
Bright, T. 1954	*The Rise of Nonconformity in the Forest of Dean* [1954].
BRSP	*Bristol Record Society Publications* (from 1930).
Caston, M. 1860	*Independency in Bristol.*
CHST	*Transactions of the Congregational Historical Society*, 21 vols (1901–72).
CYB	*The Congregational Year Book* (Congregational Union of England & Wales), from 1846.
Dolbey, G. W. 1964	*The Architectural Expression of Methodism: The First Hundred Years.*
Eayrs, G. 1911	*Wesley and Kingswood and its Free Churches.*
England, J. 1886–7	*The Western Group of Moravian Chapels ... The West of England and South Wales*, in 2 parts.
Evans, G. E. 1897	*Vestiges of Protestant Dissent.*
Ivimey, H. 1811–30	*A History of the English Baptists*, 4 vols.
Kendall, H. B. 1905	*The Origin and History of the Primitive Methodist Church*, 2 vols, [1905].
Lidbetter, H. 1961	*The Friends Meeting House.*
Lindley, K. 1969	*Chapels and Meeting Houses.*
Little, B. 1966	*Catholic Churches Since 1623.*
LRSP	*London Record Society Publications* (from 1965).
Murch, J. 1835	*A History of the Presbyterian and General Baptist Churches in the West of England.*
Oliver, R. W. 1968	*The Chapels of Wiltshire and the West*, vol. 5 of *The Strict Baptist Chapels of England* (5 vols, 1952–68).
Pevsner, N., ed. 1970	*Gloucestershire* (Buildings of England Series), Pevsner, N., ed. and Verey, D., 2 vols.
Seymour, A. C. H. 1839	*The Life and Times of Selina, Countess of Huntingdon* [Seymour, A. C. H.], 2 vols.
Sturge, C. D. *et al.* 1895	*An Account of the Charitable Trusts ... Belonging to Friends of Warwick, Leicester and Stafford Quarterly Meeting.*
Thompson, D. P. 1967	*Lady Glenorchy and Her Churches.*
VCH	Victoria History of the Counties of England, *Gloucestershire*, 6 vols (1907–81), in prog.
White, B. R. 1971–4	*Association Records of the Particular Baptists of England, Wales and Ireland to 1660*, in 3 parts (Baptist Hist. Soc.).
WHSP	*Proceedings of the Wesley Historical Society* (from 1897).
Wicks, G. H. 1910	*Free Church Life in Bristol from Wycliffe to Wesley.*

©Crown copyright 1986
First published 1986

ISBN 0 11 300008 1

Printed for HMSO by Acolortone Ltd C35 6/86 Dd.736262

Commerce and industry, which have been found to encourage independency in religious expression, were flourishing in several parts of the county in the 17th century and many societies of the older denominations came into existence at that time. Bristol, in the extreme south of the county, then a major seaport through which many groups of Puritans had left in the earlier years of the century to seek a new life in the American colonies, became the home of some of the oldest congregations; of these Broadmead (14), though lacking antiquarian interest in its buildings, makes recompense in the completeness and antiquity of its records. The woollen manufacturing area around Stroud also proved hospitable to new ideas, and travelling Quaker preachers soon attracted considerable support from amorphous groups of 'seekers' and others at Nailsworth (107), Painswick (122), and elsewhere throughout the county from Bristol (24) to Cirencester (62) and Broad Campden (55), leaving several notable meeting-houses in their wake of which those named are of particular interest. The early 19th-century meeting-house at Frenchay (162), on an older site, is also worthy of note.

The Old Baptist Chapel in Tewkesbury (145) is another reminder of a church which has existed from the mid 17th century although looking for its earliest support mainly amongst like-minded congregations to the north; the meeting-house, a converted timber-framed house hidden in a narrow alley, redolent of the clandestine meetings of a proscribed conventicle, is as enigmatic about its history as were the earlier professors about their place of meeting. A rare but slight reminder of the Seventh-day Baptists also exists nearby in the graveyard at Natton (2).

Presbyterian congregations which sprang up in many of the main centres of population following the Restoration are no longer represented by any notable chapels of that period; Barton Street Chapel, Gloucester (75), a plain brick building of 1699, entirely transformed in the late 19th century, has been demolished as has the much altered Old Chapel in Stroud (138), while the surviving Gosditch Street Chapel in Cirencester (59) also suffered a major 19th-century refitting at the hands of its Unitarian congregation. The early 18th-century Frenchay Chapel (161), however, although much altered about 1800, remains of especial importance for the provision of a prominent bell-tower above the entrance. The former chapel at Marshfield (101), of 1752, is a dignified and remarkably well-preserved building of its period, while in Bristol the rebuilt

Lewin's Mead Meeting-house (32), of 1787–91, is of national importance.

Many of the leading figures in the Evangelical Revival of the 18th century were attracted to Gloucestershire as a fruitful field of activity. George Whitefield, a native of Gloucester, was responsible for forming Methodist societies in Bristol and Kingswood, which John Wesley was soon called to administer, and on becoming the leader of Calvinistic Methodists he encouraged the growth of further societies including Kingswood (90) and Rodborough (140), both of which have 'Tabernacles' of this period, the former being of particular architectural interest. John Wesley is especially remembered at Bristol where the New Room (26), partly of 1739 though enlarged and refashioned in 1748, is the oldest remaining Methodist preaching-house. Lesser known though still historically important is the former Methodist octagon chapel in Stroud (142), of 1763, the oldest survivor of a style of building for which Wesley expressed particular favour. Captain Thomas Webb, doyen of American Methodism, was closely connected with the erection of Portland Chapel, Bristol (27), in 1791–2, a building which in its overtly parochial character proclaimed Methodism's emancipation from the Anglican attachments of its founder and which is one of the more tragic architectural losses to have occurred during the course of this survey. The Rev. Rowland Hill is also associated with this county in the Tabernacle at Wotton-under-Edge (169) although only the house remains of the 18th-century structure. The Countess of Huntingdon is more evident in her encouragement of the work of Whitefield than in the few 19th-century chapels which still bear the name of her Connexion, but the comparable though less well-known Lady Glenorchy has left as one of her rare English chapels, Hope Chapel in Bristol (19), of 1786–8. John Cennick whose brief but active life was devoted to the furtherance of Moravian societies in Wiltshire and Ireland also began his work in Gloucestershire amongst the miners of Kingswood where is one of the few chapels of this denomination in the county (93), others being at Apperley (68) and Brockweir (86).

The impetus given by these and others of lesser fame to the growth and muliplication of societies of various denominations continued into the 19th century when it is particularly evident in the mining areas of the Forest of Dean and in the vicinity of Kingswood near Bristol. In

Cheltenham the needs of visitors to a popular watering place resulted in a rich variety of chapels which were an epitome of the architecture of early 19th-century dissent; of these Salem Chapel (40), of 1844, is an interesting example of the Gothic style. Although few outstanding Gothic Revival buildings were recorded, Buckingham Chapel in Bristol (16), of 1842, is unusually important as an exceptionally early and scholarly exercise for a Baptist church, while Highbury Chapel, Bristol (22), is notable as the earliest work of William Butterfield.

The grand Classical manner, found in the late 18th-century at Lewin's Mead Meeting-house (32) and in some degree at Uley (154), is best exemplified in the following century in the chapel in Bristol (17), designed for the Catholic Apostolic Church although never used by them and an early and surprising choice for that denomination; Bedford Street Chapel, Stroud (139), of 1835–7, also in this style, has an unusual and imaginative circular stair-tower to give access to the principal floor.

The general availability of good building stone throughout the Cotswold parts of the county has ensured that many of even the smaller and plainer chapels have an intrinsic merit and blend well with their surroundings. Little early brickwork was noted, the earliest being at Barton Street, Gloucester (75), of 1699. Roofs covered with small stone slates remain in a few places but their replacement by pantiles, blue slate or more recent materials has been widespread.

ALKINGTON

(1) CONGREGATIONAL, Newport (ST 698974). Built 1825 to replace a chapel of 1710. Rendered walls and patent tile roof gabled E and W; a small vestry with stone slate roof projects to the south. Original fittings include pulpit with bowed front supported by two columns and gallery around three sides with contemporary pews.

ASHCHURCH

(2) SEVENTH-DAY BAPTIST, Natton (SO 929326). A church which met here from the 18th century or before, divided in 1871 when seceders built a new chapel at Kinsham (see Worcestershire (6)). A small building on the site which may have been the former meeting-house was demolished c.1960–70. The burial-ground enclosed by brick walls has monuments dated 1761–1947. *Communion Table*: see Tewkesbury (145).

(3) WESLEYAN, Aston Cross (SO 942340). Three bays with hipped roof, 1845.

AVENING

(4) BAPTIST (ST 884979). Built on steeply sloping site, with coursed rubble walls and hipped stone slated roof; tablet between two round-arched windows in side wall inscribed 'This Place of Worship was Erected 1805, Enlarged 1821'.

AWRE

(5) BAPTIST, Blakeney (SO 671069). Built 1835, altered and refenestrated 1874.

(6) CONGREGATIONAL, Blakeney (SO 669070). Three-bay ashlar front with pyramidal finials. Built 1849 to replace a chapel at Blakeney Hill opened 1823. (URC)
  Bright (1954) 17–18.

BERKELEY

(7) CONGREGATIONAL 'Union Chapel', Salter Street (ST 683993). Dated 1835; ashlar front with pedimental gable, two tall windows with four-centred arched heads and an open porch.

BISLEY-WITH-LYPIATT

(8) BAPTIST, Eastcombe (SO 890043). A large building of rubble with a slate roof, built in 1800–1, enlarged 1816 and greatly altered by heightening and refitting in 1860. The S front, largely of the late 19th century, is gabled and has a stone bell-cote with one bell above a clockface and two tiers of round-arched windows. Traces of earlier work in E wall include a blocked doorway with remains of windows above and to the left, with indications of an extension to the rear. The interior is divided by cast-iron arcades of five bays carrying galleries around three sides and a barrel vault over the central space.

Fittings – *Coffin Stools*: two, with enriched upper rails, early 18th-century. *Monuments*: in chapel (1) Rev. Thomas Williams, 1806, founder and first pastor, and Phebe his widow 1827; (2) Richard Faulkes, 1847, and Esther his wife 1845; (3) Henry Hook, 1833, *et al. Organ*: with Gothic case, *c*.1800, formerly at Bussage House, re-erected 1863.

The Free Churchman (Stroud District Free Church Council), June 1901–Jan. 1902.

BITTON   *Avon*

(9) CONGREGATIONAL, Upton Cheyney (ST 693701). Built 1834, much altered *c*.1900. End-entrance in semicircular porch between two round-arched windows. (URC)

Eayrs (1911) 175–7.

(10) Former WESLEYAN (ST 681697). Three-bay ashlar front with pediment, terminal pilasters, round-arched windows and obscured tablet above entrance formerly dated 1834.

BLOCKLEY

(11) Former BAPTIST (SP 16303483), now village hall. Built in 1792 for a church formed by Rev. Elisha Smith (1754–1819) and superseded by a new chapel (see below) in 1835. The walls are of coursed rubble and the roof is hipped and covered with slates. The front wall has a central doorway with moulded architrave and a tripartite lunette above with a small square tablet dated 1792 above the entrance. Two windows in the rear wall which flank the site of the pulpit have round-arched heads with keystones. The side walls are blank. The interior (26½ft by 18½ft) has a small gallery next to the entrance.

(12) BAPTIST, High Street (SP 16283480). Chapel dated 1835, replacing the foregoing, stands at the rear of a large burial-ground. The walls are of rubble with an ashlar front and the roof

is slated. The pedimented front wall is of three bays with Ionic pilasters next the corners, two plain round-arched windows and a central doorway with open pediment supported by columns and a tablet above bearing the name 'Ebenezer'. Two round-arched windows in each side wall; former British School at rear.

The interior has a plaster ceiling with moulded cornice and circular ceiling rose. A gallery above the entrance, supported by two cast-iron columns of quatrefoil section, has a front with partly open cast-iron traceried panels. The pulpit and lower seating were renewed in the late 19th century, original cast-iron gates and piers next to the street were removed *c*.1960–70. (Internal subdivision proposed 1971; reported disused 1982)

Lindley (1969), pl. 7.

BOURTON-ON-THE-WATER

(13) BAPTIST, Station Road (SP 169207). Built 1876 superseding an earlier meeting-house on another site; the front is gabled and has a large wheel window above the entrance. *Monuments*: in chapel (1) Rev. Benjamin Beddome, 1795, 50 years pastor, and Elizabeth his wife, 1784, signed Lewis, Gloster; (2) Hannah, daughter of William and Mary Palmer, 1787; (3) Rev. Thomas Coles A.M., 1840, signed H. Roff, Stow and Gardner, Cheltenham; (4) Letitia, widow of Rev. William Wilkins,

1844. Also in rear room (5) _____, 'eldest surviving daughter of Benjamin Seward of Bengworth, Worcs', late 18th-century tripartite monument with columns flanking central panel, partly concealed by inserted ceiling.

The *former meeting-house*, 400 yards E (SP 172207), built 1701, rebuilt 1765, for a church in existence by 1655, has been demolished; the surrounding burial-ground adjacent to the public cemetery is enclosed by a stone wall. *Monuments*: (1) Hannah Coller, 1713, small headstone with scrolled top and hour-glass; (2) Sarah Coller, 1713, comparable design to last, with book; (3) Mary Hartwell, 1819, and later panel above to William Hartwell, 1852 and Sarah his wife, 1850, cast-iron, signed Hartwell, Bourton; (4) Sarah (Kyte) wife of John Hall, 1803, with oval inscription panel; (5) Thomas Coles A.M., 1810, who 'preached in the adjoining place of worship for nearly forty years', Elizabeth his widow, 1836, *et al.*, capstone from table-tomb; (6) William Wood, 1794, Sarah his wife, 1776, and three children, rectangular box-tomb with pilasters, cornice, and moulded capping; (7) Benjamin Beddome, 1795, 50 years pastor, headstone erected late 19th century, probably on site of vault in chapel; (8) John Nicholas, 1703, and Joshua Head, 1739.

Oliver (1968) 114–15.

BRISTOL
Avon

(14) BAPTIST, 'Broadmead', Union Street (ST 59007335). The chapel was replaced in 1969 by a new development of shops and offices incorporating a meeting-house on the upper floors. The site N of Broadmead has been occupied since the late 17th-century by a church which originated about 1640 as an Independent society, becoming Baptist in 1653. For a few years after 1660 meetings were held in the Friars, then in Whitson Court, and in 1671 'we tooke the Meeting house at the lower end of Broadmead (where the heretics called Quakers had formerly used to meet)'. The meeting-house was desecrated in 1681 and until 1687 the congregation met in various places before returning 'to their old Meeting-place' in that year. A new meeting-house (40ft by 50ft) was built in 1695 which was sub-jected to a series of alterations and enlargements principally in 1764–5, 1871–2 and 1875, leaving a building ultimately 92ft by 50ft of which less than half of the E wall only may have formed part of the original structure. The W wall was rebuilt or refaced in 1876–7 to designs by Alfred Harford when the adjacent Lower Union Street was laid out.

BRSP XXVII (1974) 'The Records of a Church of Christ in Bristol, 1640–1687': Child, R.L. & Shipley C.E., *Broadmead Origins* (1940): Hewell, W., MS history in Bristol Record Office: Ivimey II (1814) 523–30; IV (1830) 262–83: Oliver (1968) 94–7.

(15) BAPTIST, Old King Street (ST 592734). The church which originated *c.* 1650, met first at the Friars, and in 1679 purchased land in Red Cross Street, jointly with the Broadmead church, for a burial ground. About 1699 a 'sope house' at the Pithay was converted to a meeting-house. The chapel dated 1815, demolished in 1957 after the congregation had removed to Cairns Road, had an ashlar front of three bays with a pediment and two tiers of round-arched windows.

Ivimey II (1814) 541–4; IV (1830) 283–9: Oliver (1968) 97–8.

(16) BAPTIST, 'Buckingham Chapel', Queens Road (ST 574732). Stone and slate, built 1842 to designs by R.S. Pope in French Gothic style of the late 13th century.

(17) Former CATHOLIC APOSTOLIC, Colston Avenue (ST 586731), on the W side of the former quay, was built 1839–43 to the designs of R.S. Pope. Financial difficulties amongst the promoters forced the sale of the building before completion to

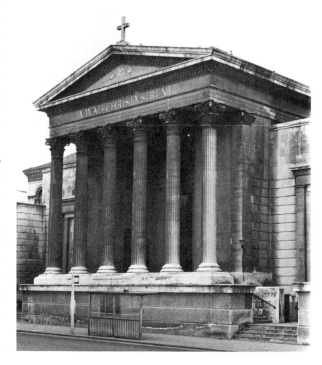

the Roman Catholics who continue to use it as the 'Church of St Mary on the Quay'. The front, of ashlar, has a central portico of six Corinthian columns supporting a pediment and two similar columns *in antis* behind. The interior has an elaborately detailed sanctuary at the W end with four columns of the same order flanking the chancel, N and S transepts, and a nave of five bays with an E gallery.

Little (1966) 75.

(18) THE TABERNACLE, Penn Street (ST 593734), demolished in 1958, was built for a Methodist society formed in 1739 which continued to support George Whitefield after his break with the Wesleys. The society met until 1753 in Smith's Hall, latterly 'Cutlers' Hall'; on 13 July in that year Whitefield laid the foundation stone of the Tabernacle which was opened on 25 November. The Calvinistic Methodist society became Congregational in the 19th century.

(A second Calvinistic Methodist society was commenced by the Countess of Huntingdon in 1775, meeting in an assembly room in St Augustine's Place; a new chapel built in Trenchard Street (ST 585731) in 1831 was demolished before 1970 after a long period in commercial use.)

Photograph © R. Winstone.

The Tabernacle appears to have been of five bays in length divided into nave and aisles by tall Tuscan columns of stone, with a coved ceiling to the nave, central octagonal lantern, and galleries around three sides. The roof was gabled to front and back, hipped down to the lantern, and with separate roofs above the side galleries. The W front of three bays with a pediment had two tiers of segmental-arched windows. The interior was partly refitted in the late 19th century but the *pulpit* (reported to be now in The Whitfield Memorial Tabernacle, Horfield, Bristol) was original and had a square base with Ionic columns at the corners, a pedimented back panel and pair of staircases. Immediately S of the chapel stood the Sunday-school of 1834 with Whitefield's house, subsequently vestries, behind.

Belden [*c*.1930] 197–8: Caston (1860) 118–27: Photographs in NMR.

(19) HOPE CHAPEL, Clifton (ST 56907265). When in 1785 Lady Glenorchy and Lady Henrietta Hope visited the Hotwells for medical treatment they determined to build a chapel for Calvinistic evangelical worship. Lady Hope died in January 1786 and Lady Glenorchy 'procured a plan for a neat place of worship, plain but elegant, and which will be a suitable monument for my dear friend Lady Henrietta, and which I mean to call Hope Chapel'. On the death of Lady Glenorchy in July 1786 the completion of the building was left to her executrix Lady Maxwell and this was achieved by the end of August 1788. Until 1820 it was a proprietary chapel with, for most of that period, liturgical services; in that year an Independent Church was formed. The establishment in 1866 of a new congregation in Oakfield Road (closed 1929) at Pembroke Chapel caused a serious decline in the support for Hope Chapel. By 1971 services were being held in a back room.

The chapel, built in 1786–8, was partly rebuilt and enlarged to the rear in 1838 at a cost of about £2,000. The present fenestration and some of the fittings are of the latter date but the seating was all renewed in the late 19th century. The original building was described by the first regular minister, William Jay, as 'a plain structure with small doors, small windows and plastered walls', the pulpit 'small and high up' and at its sides 'pews for invalids with curtains which could be drawn if need be'.

The walls are of rubble with stone dressings and the roof is hipped and slated. The S front is of four bays with panelled corner pilasters, moulded cornice, and parapet with raised centre. The side walls, originally of four bays, extended to the N by one bay, have tall windows with two-centred arched heads, divided by stone panels at gallery level; the E wall has been

rebuilt but a joint in the W wall marks the original extent of the building. At the N end is a two-storied vestry wing of 1838. The interior (now 68½ft by 48½ft; originally 48½ft square) has a gallery around four sides approached by staircases in the SE and SW corners, and an organ recess at the N end at gallery level. The roof is supported by five queen-post trusses all probably dating from 1838.

Fittings – *Monuments*: in chapel (1) S. Gell, 1848, late of Liverpool; (2) Henrietta Buchan, 1823, and Helen her sister, 1815; (3) Adamina Buchan, 1825; (4) William Hope Weir, 1811, of Craigie Hall and Blackwood in North Britain, signed Hy. Wood, Bristol; (5) Rev. W.H. Guy, 1830, ten years minister; (6) Joseph Lawrence, 1841; (7) Lady Henrietta Hope, 1786, daughter of James, Earl of Hopetown, oval tablet on grey marble backing surmounted by a plain urn; (8) Sarah, daughter of William and Rebecca Friend, 1791; (9) Mary Ann, wife of Joseph Lawrence, 1848; (10) Rev. William Gregory, 1853, 21 years pastor; (11) Henry Foster, 1819, 'sometime one of the managers of this chapel'; (12) Charles Hope Weir, 1797; (13) Catherine Henrietta Hope Weir, 1802; (14) Elizabeth Lamplow Burder, daughter of Rev. George and Sarah Burder, 1801; in vestibule, two monuments removed 1933 from Pembroke Chapel, (15) Rev. Samuel Luke, 1868, first pastor; (16) Jemima wife of Rev. Samuel Luke, 1906, authoress of 'I think when I read that sweet story of old . . .'. Also numerous monuments in burial-ground around chapel.

Organ: given 1840, reputedly from Bath Abbey. Case of three bays divided by stepped buttresses with crocketed pinnacles and cusped arch with finial over each bay; *c.*1840. Brass plate 'W.C. Vowles, Bristol, 1886'. *Pulpit, Communion Table, and Chairs*: matching set in wood with Gothic enrichment in plaster and cast iron, *c.*1838. The pulpit, octagonal on open square base with crocketed pinnacles at corners and pair of curved stairs; table, small box with white marble top; chairs, three, one with arms.

Caston (1860) 140–53: Thompson (1967) 56–61: Wicks (1910) 134–7.

(20) ZION CHAPEL, Coronation Road (ST 589720), was built 1829–30 by John Hare, a manufacturer of 'Indian matting floor cloth' and placed in trust for Independents. The walls are of rubble with stone dressings and the roof is slated. The front wall has an open loggia of five bays with four cast-iron Greek Doric

columns between end bays, a central entrance replacing two former doorways, and round-arched upper windows with a pediment above. Original galleries around three sides are supported by fluted Ionic columns; an organ-gallery was added and the seating renewed in 1878–80. There is a schoolroom below the chapel.

Caston (1860) 161–71: Cozens H.B., *The Church of the Vow* (1930).

(21) BRUNSWICK CHAPEL, Brunswick Square (ST 59257370), was built in 1834–5 for a section of the oldest Independent church in the city which then met in a chapel, rebuilt in 1815, at Castle Green (now at Green Bank Road, Easton); the secession was caused by disagreement over a ministerial appointment. After meeting for a short period in the former Pithay Chapel the seceders built Brunswick Chapel to the designs of William Armstrong. The rendered walls have two tiers of windows, the upper ones with round-arched heads, and a continuous moulded cornice and parapet. The front of three bays has a central portico with two pairs of giant Ionic columns. Prior to its closure *c.*1950 and conversion to Masonic and later to commercial use the interior had galleries around three sides with contemporary seating and a pulpit centrally against the back wall.

Caston (1860) 183–99.

(22) HIGHBURY CHAPEL, St Michael's Hill (ST 582739), built in 1842–3 for a newly-formed Independent congregation, is believed to be the earliest work of William Butterfield who later expressed his regret at having assisted in the erection of 'a schism shop'. The chapel of stone and slate in the Perpendicular Gothic style comprises an aisled nave of five bays with a polygonal chancel at the E end. A tower by E.W. Godwin was added against the S wall in 1863, the lower stages forming a transept with gallery. The N and S arcades have four-centred arches supported by octagonal piers and a dwarf clerestory with grouped quatrefoil lights. (Sold to the established church *c.*1975)

Ayres W.F., *The Highbury Story* (1963): Caston (1860) 209–18.

(23) ARLEY CHAPEL, Cheltenham Road (ST 590743), built 1854–5 by Foster and Wood for a Congregational church, has been used since 1968 by a Polish Roman Catholic congregation.

Rubble with ashlar dressings in an Italianate style having a pedimented S front with semicircular portico and clock-tower. Unaisled nave with band of clerestory lights in timber roof, transepts and apse.

Caston (1860) 225–33: *CYB* (1857) 241–2.

(24) Former FRIENDS, Quakers Friars (ST 593733). The first meeting-house on this site was built in 1670 superseding a building 'at the lower end of Broadmead' which then passed into the hands of the Baptists. In 1681, together with the meeting-houses of other denominations, the building was despoiled but later repaired and registered as a place of worship 12 August 1689. An illustration on James Millerd's Plan of Bristol (1673) shows a building of three bays and two tiers of windows at the S end, perhaps square on plan, with a hipped roof surmounted by a lantern. It apparently faced W and from 1701 had a burial-ground to the east. The present meeting-house, sold in 1956 and now serving as a Registry office, was built in 1747–9 on the earlier foundations to designs by George Tully, a member of the society, but with additional details attributed to Thomas Paty. A separate smaller meeting-house was added alongside in 1759.

The principal meeting-house, dated 1747, has rendered walls and a flat lead roof with hipped slated roofs surrounding a central lantern; the walls have a low plinth and plain platband and rise without a cornice to a parapet with simply moulded coping which sweeps up slightly at each corner of the building. The windows, which are in two tiers, have moulded stone architraves with segmental-arched heads and keystones. The broad E front of three bays has a central doorway with pediment and triple keystone. The N and S walls have each three principal bays

of windows and a fourth eastern bay with an external doorway, now closed, and a window above to light the gallery stairs. The W wall is blank and partly covered by earlier buildings.

The interior (46ft by 60½ft) has galleries around the N, S and E sides with fielded panelled fronts and stairs in the NE and SE corners (the former now removed). The square central space in front of the galleries is bounded on three sides by tall Roman Doric columns of stone with high plinths, two columns on each side being free-standing with half-columns against the W wall and grouped columns in the opposite corners. Centrally in the ceiling is a square lantern with one window in each face and a balustraded opening (now closed at ceiling level). The fittings were mostly removed on conversion but some seating remains in the gallery. The stand with three tiers of seating was against the W wall with two ranks of seating facing towards it which were originally described as comprising eight seats each side of a central aisle, the two pairs of seats at the front being narrower than the rest and having each 'a sliding seat to draw out 14in.'.

A *burial-ground* in Redcliff Way, 'Redcliff Pit' (ST 590724), used by this society 1665–1923 was converted in 1950 to a public garden; the front boundary wall and flat rectangular marker-stones were then removed. In the natural rock face on the E side is a mediaeval stone arch.

Architectural Review, April 1946: *BRSP* XXVI (1971); XXVII (1973); XXX (1977): Lidbetter (1961) 73: Wicks (1910) 59.

(25) Former FRIENDS, Kings Weston Road (ST 549782). A small meeting in existence by 1670 was reported in 1710 to be in need of larger premises. The erection of a new meeting-house was notified to Yearly Meeting in 1713 although the present building, which is dated 1718 above the entrance, was not conveyed to trustees until April 1718. Meetings ceased in 1893 and the property was sold in 1924.

The former meeting-house (22¾ft by 36¼ft externally), now divided between two houses adjoining N and W, 'Quakers Rest' and 'Ferns Hill', has rendered rubble walls and a hipped roof covered with patent tiles. The S front, of three bays, has a central entrance and flanking windows with moulded stone architraves; a fanlight was inserted above the doorway in the early 19th century.

Mounting Steps: E of meeting-house, 18th-century.

A *burial-ground* in Kings Weston Lane (ST 540780) given to the society in 1690 is a rectangular walled enclosure with 18th-century gateway at the SW end.

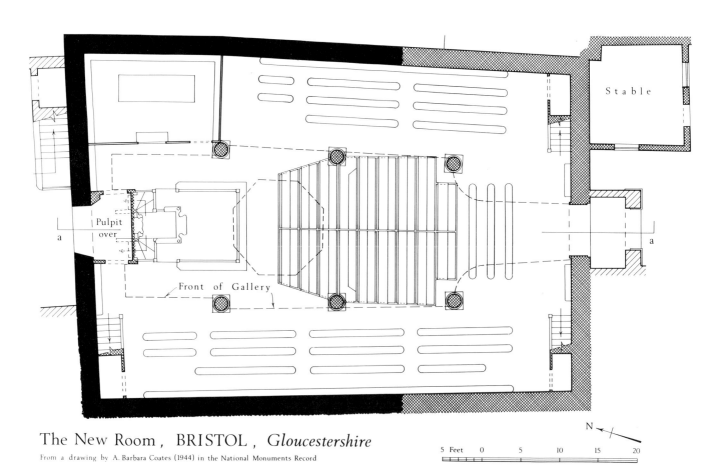

Pulpit
over

a   a

Front of Gallery

Stable

The New Room , BRISTOL , *Gloucestershire*

From a drawing by A. Barbara Coates (1944) in the National Monuments Record

N

5 Feet   0   5   10   15   20

N front.

Interior from S.
(26) BRISTOL. The New Room, Broadmead and The Horsefair.

(26) THE NEW ROOM, Broadmead and The Horsefair (ST 59107338), was first built in 1739 to accommodate certain religious societies formerly meeting in Nicholas St and Baldwin St. These societies had been fostered by George Whitefield, but on his departure for America their oversight passed to John Wesley. Wesley records the laying of the first stone on 12 May 1739. The building, which became a principal centre for Methodist activity, was greatly enlarged and much rebuilt in 1748 although parts of the N and E walls probably remain from the earlier structure. The society at the New Room was weakened in 1792 by the opening of Portland Chapel, where Wesley's rigid policy over ministerial qualifications for the administration of communion was not accepted, and in 1794 a major division occurred over this issue resulting in the erection of Old King Street Chapel. In 1808 the New Room was sold to Welsh Calvinistic Methodists who retained possession until 1929; it was then repurchased by Wesleyan Methodists and restored under the guidance of Sir George Oatley.

The building, which has rendered walls and hipped pantiled roofs, stands on a site formerly concealed by surrounding buildings; it comprises a galleried chapel and a series of small rooms on a floor above which served the needs of John and Charles Wesley and their assistants. The original entrance from the Horsefair was by a narrow alley at the NE corner of the building opening to a small court against the N wall. The principal entrance was removed to the opposite end when the building was extended to the S in 1748. The external walls make little attempt at architectural pretension. A segmental-arched doorway at the centre of the N wall with a similarly-arched window above may be part of the original design; an attenuated window in the E wall may also relate to the earlier building. At the S end is a central entrance with round-arched window above and domestic windows to the upper floor.

The interior, of irregular plan, (approx. 63ft by 42ft) with separate E and W galleries and six tall Tuscan columns of stone supporting the upper floor, has a pulpit centrally at the N end and an octagonal lantern in the ceiling which rises through the upper storey. A small vestry or 'Conference Room' in which many of Wesley's early conferences were held occupies the NE corner of the lower floor. The upper rooms are ranged around three sides of a central common room which is lit by two windows in the S wall and by the central lantern.

Fittings – *Clock*: on front of W gallery, with shaped case and circular dial, early 18th-century. *Inscription*: on stone, externally in N wall near NE corner, 'THE REV: Mr. J : WESLEY AM : LD : THS STONE AD1739' (surname and degree altered). *Organ*: in gallery, small chamber organ by John Snetzler, 1761, from Little Plumstead Church, Norfolk, given 1930. *Poor-box*: on outer face of N door, brass plate with slot inscribed with texts from Mark x.21 and Prov. xiv.21 and date 1755. *Pulpit*: two desks with panelled front and balustraded staircases, approached from gallery only; lower desk 18th-century, upper desk a replica of *c*. 1930 to replace one removed when an organ was sited here in the 19th century. *Seating*: box-pews to lower floor, early 19th-century, also plain benches some of 18th-century date. *Miscellaneous*: many items of general Methodist interest are exhibited in the upper rooms.

Dolbey (1964) 41–3: Edwards M., *The New Room* (1972).

(27) PORTLAND CHAPEL (ST 585738) was built 1791–2 to serve Methodists living in the new residential districts N of the city centre and to relieve the pressure on the 'New Room'. One of the principal supporters of the new cause was Captain Thomas Webb who was earlier notable for his part in introducing Methodism to America and who is buried in the chapel.

The walls are of rubble and brick with a rendered surface and the roof is slated. Prior to 1871–2, when the building was extended by one bay to the W, the original entrances closed and a polygonal organ-chamber erected against the N wall, the N and S walls were symmetrical. These were of five bays with a slightly projecting pedimented centre of three bays with an entrance in the middle bay and round-arched windows with keystones and impost blocks. The N pediment has been removed but that to the S remains and has within it a circular panel. At the E end is a lower vestry wing with hipped lean-to roof, and at the W end, extended in a similar style, an original octagonal wooden bell-cote with weather-vane dated 1792 has been reset above the later gable.

The interior (originally 55½ft by 39ft) has a plaster ceiling with a wide cove along the principal sides. At the E end is a small apse with arched opening to the chapel and an upper arch

Portland Chapel, BRISTOL
Gloucestershire

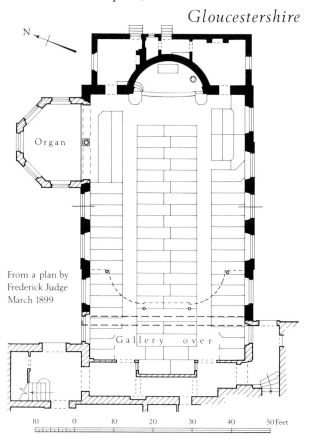

N

Organ

From a plan by
Frederick Judge
March 1899

Gallery over

10   0   10   20   30   40   50 Feet

S wall.

Interior from W.
(27) BRISTOL. Portland Chapel.

springing from the line of the cornice at the base of the ceiling. A gallery at the W end with concave panelled front was re-sited one bay W of its former position when the chapel was extended. The seating, of panelled box-pews in three ranks, was altered in 1864, prior to which it comprised two principal ranks with a centre aisle. The pulpit and reading desk, formerly combined as a central feature with a communion table behind them in the apse, were re-sited further E in 1864 when the table was brought forward; they were subsequently divided and placed N and S of the apse.

The original decorative scheme at the E end, now entirely obliterated, is reported to have comprised within the apse 'a scene of tropical vegetation, the centre foreground being occupied by a tomb or sepulchre surmounted by an urn' with 'three winged cherubs' heads' in the clouds above. On the wall around the arched opening, presumably below the upper arch, 'were painted crimson curtains draped back'. The latter were painted out in 1913 but the former, in spite of a proposal in 1872 to substitute the traditional tables of Lord's prayer, creed and decalogue, remained, although possibly retouched, until more recent years. The painting has been ascribed to Edward Bird R.A.

Other fittings include – Bell: in bell-cote, reported to be dated 1698, formerly at St Ewen's Church, Broad St., Bristol. Font: stone or composition octagonal pillar with tapered panelled stem, moulded base and bowl, late 18th-century. Monuments: in chapel, on N wall (1) Thomas Foster junior B.A., architect, 1846, and Sophia his widow, 1874; (2) Mary (Stoakes) Coleman, 1795, recording a bequest of £100; in E wall (3) Lieut. (Captain) Thomas Webb, 1796, 'the principal instrument in erecting this chapel'; (4) Rev. James Wood, 1840, 67 years Wesleyan minister, and Mary his wife, 1832; on S wall (5) John Hall, gent., 1798, preacher; (6) Rev. Joseph Collier, 1842, and Sarah his widow, 1851; on W wall (7) Rev. Thomas Roberts A.M., 1832; (8) Rev. John Sugden Smith, 1825; on S wall of vestry, externally (9) Thomas Westell, 1794; also many monuments in burial-ground to S and east. Burial-vaults below chapel include, below apse, 'Captain Webb's Vault, 1796'. (Chapel closed 1970–1 and since demolished. Bell removed to Victoria Chapel, Whiteladies Road, Bristol. Remains of Captain Webb and his wife reburied at New Room 1972; his monument (3) removed to John Street Chapel, New York, U.S.A., 1973)

Lambert, A.J., *The Chapel on the Hill* (1929): *WHSP* XXXVIII (Aug. 1972) 127–30; XXXIX (Oct. 1973) 57–60.

(28) EBENEZER CHAPEL, Old King Street (ST 591734) on the W side of the street (now 'Merchant Street'), 80 yards N of the New Room, was built in 1794–5 for a Wesleyan society formed by secession from the New Room. This followed the refusal of the trustees to allow preaching by a minister without episcopal ordination who had assisted in administering the Lord's Supper at Portland Chapel. The chapel had a front of five bays with a pediment, shaped parapet and two tiers of round-arched windows. The interior, partly refitted in 1859, had a gallery around four sides, rounded at the back. (Closed and demolished 1954)

Lambert, *op. cit.*, 23–5: *WHSP* XXIX (1954) 124–30: Williams T.M., *A Short History of Old King Street (Ebenezer) Methodist Church, Bristol* (1954).

(29) WESLEYAN, British Road (ST 582714). Late 19th-century; formerly with four giant columns supporting a pediment between staircase wings, now entirely transformed by partial demolition and refitting. The former 'Ebenezer Chapel' of 1836 alongside (derelict 1977) has rendered walls and a slate roof hipped to the front. The front wall is of three bays with a pedimented centre bay and a simplified Venetian window above the central round-arched entrance.

(30) ZION CHAPEL, Two Mile Hill Road (ST 644739). Free Methodist, dated 1854.

(31) MORAVIAN, Upper Maudlin Street (ST 587734). Land on the E side of the street was bought in 1756 by a recently formed congregation and a chapel built which was opened in 1757; a burial-ground behind the chapel was surrounded by related buildings including, on the N side, a minister's house, a sisters' house and girls' school, and on the E the cooperage house (rebuilt 1863–4 as day and Sunday-schools) and the brethren's house. About 1827 the roof and ceiling of the chapel were rebuilt and in 1854 it was reseated and the pulpit 'exchanged for one of a chaster and more modern style'. In 1871 the street was widened and its level raised, involving the removal of some buildings which had stood partly in front of the chapel, notably a manse built in 1853 which was then replaced by another alongside the first minister's house N of the chapel. Some further alterations to the chapel were made in 1875 but in 1896 a more drastic change was made involving substantial rebuilding to provide a new chapel at the street level with a hall below.

The chapel, of which the lower part of the walls dates from 1756–7, has rendered walls with a brick superstructure and tiled roof. The original building had rusticated quoins and tall segmental-arched windows with rusticated surrounds, of four bays to E and W; these features remain but the windows have been reduced in height. At the N end is a small doorway with keystone which gave access from the minister's house. The upper chapel ($54\frac{1}{2}$ft by 30ft) has at the S end a re-used gallery of *c.*1757 with bowed centre supported by two Tuscan columns; in the gallery is an early 19th-century organ. The pulpit of 1854 is semi-octagonal with an arched back-board, dentil cornice to the upper stage and a low reading desk in front: *Glass*: in circular window above pulpit, includes symbol of Lamb and Flag (now in St Nicholas Church Museum). *Monuments*: in burial-ground, many rectangular marker-stones, re-sited 1955, (1) Elizabeth Skrine, 1763; (2) Mary Moor, 1777; (3) Sarah Bell, 1780; the latest stone visible, to Bishop George Macleary, is dated 1963. (Site sold for redevelopment 1971)

England II (1887) 2–4, pls. XIV, IV.

(32) LEWIN'S MEAD MEETING-HOUSE (ST 58687332). A Presbyterian congregation was in existence in Bristol by 1672 in which year John Weeks, ejected Vicar of Buckland Newton, Dorset, was licensed as a 'teacher' and 'a room or rooms in the house of John Lloyd, lying on St James's Back' was allowed as a

S front.

Interior from S.
(32) BRISTOL. Lewin's Mead Meeting-house.

meeting place. This place remained in use until December 1681 when the contents were destroyed and the congregation forced to meet elsewhere. A permanent meeting-house was next obtained in 1686 by the conversion of a theatre in Tucker Street, S of Bristol bridge, but a rapid growth in the society appears to have necessitated the provision of a second place of worship in the N part of the town in 1693–4. The two congregations formed a single society at least until the death of Weeks in 1698 but had divided by the early 18th century when the former is credited with 500 and the latter with 1,600 hearers. The Tucker Street society, which built a new chapel in Bridge Street in 1786, remained largely orthodox, becoming Congregational before 1868 when it removed to Clifton Down. The society at Lewin's Mead which supported the contrary position became generally regarded as Unitarian by the early 19th century.

The meeting-house built in 1693–4 on the NW side of Lewin's Mead was demolished in 1787 and the present building erected on the same site was registered 1 September 1791. It then included stables and coach-house to which were added in 1818 a lecture-room above the stables and in 1826 two large school-rooms, a committee room, kitchen and a 'small tenement' for the master and mistress of the infant school and the mistress of the girls' day school.

The chapel, designed by William Blackburn of London, has walls of rendered rubble with ashlar dressings and ashlar facing to the front wall above a rusticated lower stage; the principal roof is hipped and covered with slates. The body of the chapel is a broad rectangle with a projecting pedimented centrepiece to the S having an open semicircular porch with paired Ionic columns and, above it, a large tripartite window with arched head which is repeated centrally at the E and W ends of the building and as a row of three on the N side. The re-entrant corners at the front are occupied by staircase wings which rise in two stages to the level of the springing of the arches of the principal windows.

The interior (45ft by 70ft excluding front bay), although superficially redecorated in the late 19th century, retains most of its original fittings. The ceiling is divided into panels and ornamented by six large ceiling roses. Galleries at the E and W ends are approached independently by semicircular stone stair-cases, linked by a third gallery to the S which is occupied by the organ and singers' seats; the galleries have plain fronts with late 19th-century ornament and are supported by cast-iron columns.

The *pulpit*, centrally against the N wall is of mahogany with a square panelled desk with chamfered corners rising from a flared base, a panelled back-board and semicircular canopy surmounted by an urn; to the W is a desk for the chapel clerk and in front is a segmental communion-rail with turned balusters; the con-temporary communion table is now in the vestry. Inside the principal S entrance is a semicircular lobby, formerly smaller with an inner passage between it and the tall ends of the adjacent pews; these have now been conflated and the pew ends raised to full height. The seating to the lower floor comprises a full set of box-pews, with seats for doorkeepers directly accessible from the staircase lobbies; in the E and W galleries are box-pews with some open benches in the latter and in the S gallery.

Other fittings include – *Boundary Stones*: below W window of S wall, two, marking boundary between parishes of St James and St Michael. *Collecting Shovels*: mahogany, with oval box and single handle. *Monuments*: in chapel on N wall (1) Lant Carpenter D.D., pastor, 1840; (2) Mary Carpenter, 1877. *Paintings*: oil portraits of three ministers, including Rev. William Richards, minister 1731–68, and Rev. William James, minister 1842–76. *Plate*: includes four two-handled cups and four plates of 1727; also two (formerly six) bottles of dark green Bristol glass which served in place of flagons.

Burial-Ground, Brunswick Square (ST 59287375), is entered on the N side of the square through an arch flanked by Doric columns between a pair of lodges. In the centre of the ground is a small square mortuary chapel with rendered walls and gabled roof. *Monuments*: in the chapel (1) Rev. John Prior Estlin, 1817, and Susanna (Bishop) his widow, 1842; (2) Ann, widow of Rev. Thomas Wright, 1814, and Daniel their son, 1810; (3) Rev. Thomas Wright, 1797; (4) Anne Shurmer, 1789, *et al.*, (5) William Lloyd, 1842, and Betty Elizabeth his wife, 1837; in burial-ground (6) John Latimer, author of *Annals of Bristol History*, 1904, *et al.*; (7) Elizabeth, wife of William Bonner, 1787; (8) Rev. James Davis, 'late Pastor of the Congregation of Protestant Dissenters in Bridge Street', 1797, and Mary his widow, 1814; (9) Amy Perry, 1785, monument with weeping infant and urn in bas relief.

BRSP XXVII, 74–5: Caston (1860) 80–9: Evans (1897) 35–6: Murch (1835) 99–135: *UHST* IV (1927–30) 287–9; VI (1935–8) 116–29.

CAM

(33) CONGREGATIONAL, Upper Cam (ST 757992). Built *c*.1702 on a newly acquired site for a congregation originally regarded as Presbyterian; it was much altered in 1818. The walls are of rubble and the roof which is half-hipped is covered with patent

tiles. The broad N front formerly had doorways in the end bays, one is now altered to a window. The S wall, which now has windows arranged as at the front, retains traces of two earlier windows which flanked a central pulpit, and of a blocked door-way to a vestry built in 1790 but since removed. Two bays of windows in the end walls have been partly covered at the E end by Sunday-schools added in 1895.

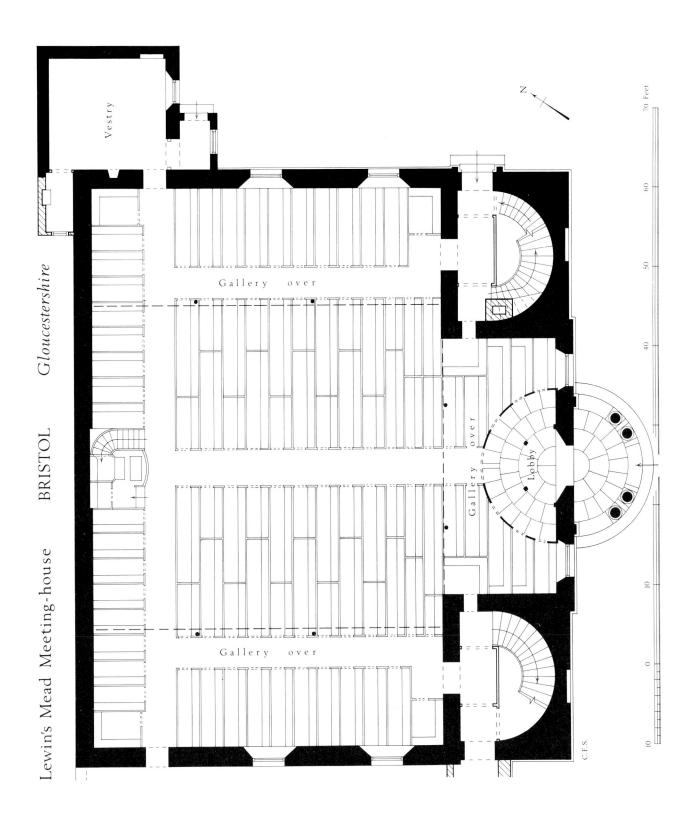

Lewin's Mead Meeting-house   BRISTOL   Gloucestershire

Vestry

Gallery over

Gallery over

Gallery over

Lobby

N

C.F.S.

10   0   10   40   50   60   70 Feet

The interior (30¼ft by 45ft) was refitted in 1818 and the pulpit re-sited at the E end. The seating was renewed in the late 19th century. The ceiling has a coved plaster cornice. Galleries around three sides, rounded to the W, were added in 1818 and are supported by cast-iron columns.

Fittings – *Clock*: on front of W gallery, with shaped face, repainted, early 18th-century. *Monuments*: in chapel (1) Alexander Baine of Dursley, mercer, 1749, and Alice his wife, 1740, marble tablet in stone surround with swan-neck pediment and egg-and-dart enrichment; (2) Rev. Joseph Twemlow, first minister, 1740, recording that the meeting-house at Water Street, Dursley, was erected at his sole expense jointly for the use of the minister of Cam meeting and for the education of forty poor children; (3) Rev. Thomas Griffith, 21 years minister, 1855, and Ann (Ballinger) his wife, 1823; (4) Rev. John Thomas, 40 years pastor, 1816, and Mary his widow, 1840; (5) Samuel White, 1816, Eleanor his wife, 1795, *et al.*; (6) Charles Whittard, 1830, Elizabeth his wife, 1802, and three children; in burial-ground N of chapel (7) William Harding of Lower Mill, 1793, Dorothy his widow, 1800, *et al.*, pedestal-tomb with oval inscription panels on each face; also six brass tablets on ledger-stones, including (8) George Minett, 1728, and George his son, 1722. *Pulpit*: reeded and panelled with bowed front above trumpet-shaped stem, *c.*1818. *Plate*: includes a pewter plate with overall decoration and the name Lydia Purnel and date 1673.

Davis, R.A., *The Up-to-Date History of Cam Meeting Congregational Church* (1962).

(34) WESLEYAN, Chapel Street, Lower Cam (SO 751003). Three-bay front with two tiers of large round-arched windows. Dated 1825; tablet at rear inscribed 'ENLARGED 1838'.

CHALFORD

(35) BAPTIST, Coppice Hill (SO 901027). The Tabernacle, by J. Tait of Leicester, was built in 1873. The former meeting-house which remains at the lower end of the burial-ground was built *c.*1740 when the church was formed but has been much altered by enlargement to the front *c.*1810 and by the addition at one end of a long Sunday-school wing.

The original building has rubble walls and a hipped roof covered with patent tiles. The rear wall retains traces of two tall windows which flanked the pulpit, now replaced by other windows at two levels; the lower ones occupy in part the sites of the earlier openings. The SE end wall has the remains of two three-light mullioned windows at ground and gallery level and the outline of the base of a double gable below the present eaves. In *c.*1810 this wall was extended at an angle and a round-arched upper window inserted centrally to the enlarged end. The front, of the early 19th century, is of three bays with two tiers of round-arched windows with Y-tracery and a central doorway altered in the late 19th century to form a carriage or stable entrance. The interior (formerly about 16ft by 31½ft) has no original features. The Sunday-school wing, of slightly later date than the enlarged chapel, has three similar upper windows and an oval tablet inscribed 'CHALFORD TABERNACLE SUNDAY SCHOOL ROOM.'

Monuments: In front of former chapel (1) Rev. James Deane, 50 years pastor, 1857, and Elizabeth his wife, 1840, with brass inscription plate; at rear (2) Daniel M . . ., minister, ?1760, headstone.

(36) CONGREGATIONAL, France Lynch (SO 898030). A 'new erected house at Chalford' was registered in 1695 for Presbyterians and a meeting existed in the early 18th century at Chalford Bottoms with Theodore Westmacott as minister. The present chapel, inscribed 'FRANCE MEETING REBUILT 1819', is a large and prominent building of stone with a hipped tiled roof (formerly stone). The S front has a wide round-arched central doorway with a small blind-glazed Venetian window above and two tiers of round-arched windows in the end bays which are repeated, in four bays, in the side walls. A lower Sunday-school wing was built against the E side in 1854.

The interior has a gallery around three sides. The seating was renewed in the late 19th century but the pulpit, apart from the staircase, is of *c.*1819.

Fittings – *Brass*: refixed to front of pulpit, small tablet inscribed 'V.D.M./Theodorus Westmacote/Obijt 31ᵐᵒ Aug.ᵗⁱ 1728.' *Monuments*: in chapel (1) John Innell, clothier, 1806, Mary his widow 1813, and three children, double monument with shields; (2) Henry Ballinger, clothier, 1785, *et al.*, double monument with shields below. Also, in burial-ground, monuments of early 19th century and later, some with brass inscription plates.

(37) PRIMITIVE METHODIST, Chalford Hill (SO 897031). Greatly altered; large tablet inscribed with two verses of a hymn and 'BUILT AD 1823 REBUILT AD 1824'.

Kendall (1905) II, 296.

CHEDWORTH

(38) Former CONGREGATIONAL, Pancakehill (SP 069111). Built 1804 to replace a meeting-house of 1752. Square building with rubble walls and a pyramidal slate roof. The SE front has a central porch, added in the mid 19th century. Two paired lancet windows at rear flank the pulpit. There is a single gallery at the

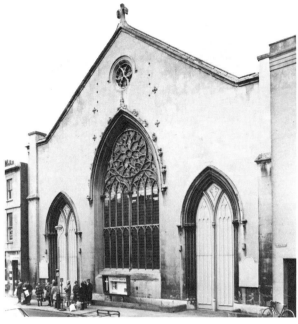

entrance, other fittings date from the late 19th century.

Monuments: in burial-ground against SW wall, two table-tombs with brass inscription tablets (1) Rev. Stephen Philipps, 36 years pastor 'in whose time and by whose exertions principally the adjoining place of worship was erected . . . ', 1836, and Mary his widow 1839; (2) Mary, (first) wife of Rev. S. Philipps, 1829; also several late 18th-century headstones with border enrichment. (Converted to domestic use and monuments removed *c*.1980)

CHELTENHAM

(39) Former BAPTIST, Knapp Road (SO 94572260). 'Bethel Chapel', facing St James's Square, was built in 1820 for a section of the Tewkesbury church which became autonomous in 1753 having met from 1690 in a former malthouse and from 1703 in a small meeting-house probably on the present site. The church, weakened by secessions in 1835 and 1866, closed the chapel in 1951 which has since been used by Mormons and Christadelphians.

The chapel has brick walls with an ashlar front and slate roof. Pedimented front of three bays with two tiers of windows enclosed in round-arched recesses.

Oliver (1968) 103–6.

(40) BAPTIST, Clarence Parade (SO 94782242). 'Salem Chapel' was built in 1844 for the 1835 seceders from 'Bethel Chapel' who first met in a picture gallery in Clarence Street and subsequently converted an existing building in Regent Street which they named 'Salem'. The chapel has a gabled front of ashlar with giant pointed-arched entrances flanking a large traceried window with crocketed label. Terminal buttresses were formerly surmounted by pinnacles. The interior has a gallery around four sides with arcaded panelled front supported by iron columns and a carved stone pulpit. The gallery, now rendered unusable by an inserted ceiling, retains its original box-pews.

The *former Chapel* in Regent Street (SO 94902225) stands behind other buildings on the E side of the street. It was built in the early 19th century as Barrett's Riding School and opened as a chapel on 1 January 1836. It is now a warehouse. Brick and slate

Interior before alteration.

with the principal S front facing Ormond Place, having a narrow doorway off-centre to the right replacing a wider entrance; when the building was converted a three-centred arched window with intersecting glazing bars was inserted at this end and three pointed-arched windows at the N end replaced earlier openings.

Blake (1979) 24: Oliver (1968) 105–6.

(41) BAPTIST, Cambray Place (SO 95032224), by H. Dangerfield the borough surveyor. Built in 1853–5 for a section of the Salem church which seceded in 1843 and met temporarily in 'The Tabernacle', Clare Street (43) and 'Ebenezer Chapel', King Street (48). The chapel has a pedimented ashlar front of three principal bays with sub-pediments to the side bays and two tiers of grouped round-arched windows. The side walls are of brickwork.

Oliver (1968) 105–6.

(42) GAS GREEN CHAPEL, Russell Street (SO 94252318), was built c.1836 to replace a chapel on a site required for the erection of the gas-works; it has been used by various denominations including Primitive Methodists, Independents from c.1848, and latterly by Baptists. The walls are rendered and the front of three bays has a low gable and two tiers of windows separated by a platband; the upper front windows have round-arched heads with keystones.

A History of Gas Green Chapel, Cheltenham, 1849–1949 [1949]: Blake (1979) 25.

(43) Former CHAPEL, Clare Street (SO 94762122), latterly in commercial use, was built in the early 19th century as 'The Tabernacle' and briefly used in 1843 by Baptist seceders from 'Salem Chapel'. Brick with rendered pedimented front and two large round-arched windows flanking altered entrance. (Demolished since 1971).

Blake (1979) 24–5: Oliver (1968) 105–6.

(44) Former CALVINISTIC METHODIST, High Street (SO 94682263). 'Cheltenham Chapel', designed by Edward Smith, was built in 1808–9 for services 'conducted on the plan of Lady Huntingdon's chapels'. The cause was weakened by the formation of other societies and in spite of re-organization in 1851 as a Congregational church the chapel was closed in 1857. It was re-opened in the following year for a congregation of the Presbyterian Church in England (now URC) which removed in 1886 to Fauconberg Road (52) and has since been used as a hall by the Salvation Army (which bought it in 1894), as a furniture store, and latterly as a wine store.

The former chapel, on the S side E of Ambrose Street, has brick walls rendered at the N end and a hipped slate roof. The N front has rusticated quoins and a platband which continues around the building; the central entrance is tall with a round-arched head and is flanked by arched recesses enclosing two tiers

of windows. The side wall to the W is of four bays with similar fenestration. A low Sunday-school wing is attached to S end. The interior, although altered by the insertion of a floor, retains the original gallery structure around three sides supported by reeded cast-iron columns with acanthus capitals. There is a coved plaster ceiling. A small burial-ground to the E contains some 19th-century headstones.

Hart, W., *A History of St Andrew's Presbyterian Church, Cheltenham* (1966): Seymour (1839) I, 440.

(45) PORTLAND CHAPEL, North Place (SO 951227), was built in 1816 by Robert Capper, previously a supporter of 'Cheltenham Chapel', who appointed Thomas Snow, a former Anglican, as minister. After Snow adopted Strict Baptist views, Capper resumed control of the chapel, giving it to the Countess of Huntingdon's trustees who re-opened it 27 June 1819. The

walls are of ashlar and the roof is hipped and slated. The front has a pointed-arched doorway and a porch, added 1865, with paired Roman Doric columns; two tiers of windows in pointed-arched recesses with basement windows below continue around the side walls.

Blake (1979) 9: Seymour (1839) I, 440.

(46) Former CHAPEL, Grosvenor Street (SO 95232223), was built in 1817–18 for the Rev. Thomas Snow after his removal from 'Portland Chapel' and used for Strict Baptist services until 1822 when Snow reverted to the Church of England and handed the building over to Anglican trustees. In 1827 it was sold to Congregationalists who re-opened it as 'Highbury Chapel', named after the London residence of Thomas Wilson the denominational benefactor. With the opening of a new chapel in Winchcombe Street in 1852 (superseded 1934 by the present chapel in Priory Walk) it became a Sunday-school and latterly a youth club.

The walls are of brick and the E front is rendered in stucco. Five bays with three-bay centre having a raised pediment above blind panels and swept parapets above the recessed wings. Round-arched upper windows above altered lower openings. The interior has a segmental barrel-vault with traces of a circular cupola at the centre; galleries around three sides with mid 19th-century cast-iron fronts.

Blake (1979) 9–10: *CYB* (1853) 255–6.

(47) Former FRIENDS, Clarence Street (SO 947225). A meeting-house built in 1836 on the S side of the then Manchester Walk was superseded in 1902–3 by the present meeting-house in Portland Street and is now part of St Paul's College Adult Education Centre. An earlier meeting-house of 1702 which stood on an adjoining site to the W was subsequently used by Unitarians,

Baptists and Primitive Methodists; It was demolished in the late 19th century.

The surviving building of 1836 has brick walls faced to the N with ashlar. Prior to *c*.1902, when an upper floor was added, it was of a single storey with a front of five bays the three centre-bays slightly recessed and fronted by a lower porch, and a secondary entrance at the W end.

Blake (1979) 3–4, 24.

(48) Former WESLEYAN 'Ebenezer Chapel', King Street (SO 94462284). Methodist meetings commenced in 1764 when a chapel in Albion Street, built in 1723 by a Presbyterian, Mr Millet, was re-opened for their use. This was later abandoned from decay and another meeting-house of *c*.1730, also reputedly Presbyterian, in Meaking's Passage off High Street, was taken instead. The chapel in King Street, was built for this congregation in 1812–13 and after being superseded in 1840 by that in St George's Street (49) was used by Baptists and from 1859–1934 by Primitive Methodists; it is now in commercial use.

The chapel has rendered brick walls with stone dressings. The S front has a narrow pedimented centre bay between wide wings

with swept parapets and short rusticated quoins at the corners. A large tablet below the pediment carries the chapel name with the denomination erased, and the date 1812. A small Doric porch has been removed.

Blake (1979) 4, 8–9: Judge G.H. Bancroft, *The Origin . . . of Wesleyan Methodism in Cheltenham* (1912): *WHSP* XII (1919–20) 180–91.

(49) WESLEYAN, St George's Street (SO 94752279). The successor to 'Ebenezer Chapel' was built in 1839–40. It is a large building of brick, partly rendered, with an ashlar front and hipped slate roof. The W front is of five bays with plinth, platband and entablature. The three middle bays project slightly and have round-arched upper windows and an inscription in raised lettering on the frieze above with the date 1839 and name 'WESLEY CHAPEL'. A portico of four Roman Doric columns

has been removed and the entrances drastically altered *c*.1960. The flanking bays have two tiers of round-arched recesses. The side walls, divided horizontally by brick platbands, have two

tiers of round-arched windows in five bays above a range of windows to a basement storey. At the E end is a gabled projection with wide lunette at the upper level incorporating a circular traceried panel perhaps from the former communion window.

The interior (61¾ft by 49¼ft) has a flat plaster ceiling with a moulded cornice and a barrel-vault above the organ loft. The E end has been altered and formerly had a communion recess behind the pulpit lit by a circular window filled with painted glass, and a separate choir gallery above. A gallery around three sides of the chapel with altered front is rounded at the W end and is supported by cast-iron columns. SE of the chapel is a school-room built in 1901 and in the NE angle is a multi-storey wing with additional classrooms also of a relatively late date. The basement is occupied by small rooms for class meetings and Sunday-school use.

Fittings – *Font*: painted wood, octagonal with panelled stem, flared base and top, incorporating blue and white pottery bowl decorated with Classical scenes and having maker's initials TT in a Staffordshire knot; early 19th-century. *Monuments*: in chapel on E wall, all by Wingate of Gloucester, (1) Robert Middleton, 1856, and Hannah his wife, 1845; (2) Mary daughter of Richard Taylor, 1856, her sister Helen Elizabeth Wheeler, 1866, and brother John, 1872; (3) Frances Maria wife of Rev. Samuel Walker, 1857. *Pulpits*: (1) at E end, rostrum incorporating parts of original octagonal pulpit; (2) loose in chapel, octagonal, early 19th-century. *Seating*: late 19th-century pews to lower floor; later theatre-type seats in gallery. (Chapel closed 1971, now in commercial use)

(50) WESLEYAN, Great Norwood Street (SO 94552135). Brick with ashlar front and slate roof, built 1845–6, replacing a smaller chapel which stood to the south. Gabled front of three bays with windows in recessed panels between stepped corner buttresses

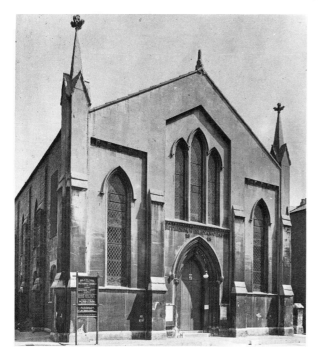

with gabled pinnacles. Pinnacles altered and inscription above entrance 'BETHESDA WESLEYAN CHAPEL' now removed.

Blake (1979) 26.

(51) Former WESLEYAN METHODIST ASSOCIATION, Regent Street (SO 950224). Built c.1840 as 'Bethany Chapel' and super-seded in 1865 by the 'Royal Well Chapel'. Plain low building with rendered W front, blank except for a round-arched door-way with fanlight near the S end, and slate roof pierced by a roof-light on the E slope. Now used by the Brethren and renamed 'Regent Chapel'.

Blake (1979) 25.

(52) PRESBYTERIAN, St Andrew's, Fauconberg Road (SO 951218). Built 1885–6 for the congregation from 'Cheltenham Chapel' (44): rock-faced stone with corner tower and spire in Gothic style by Thomas Arnold. (URC)

(53) BAYSHILL CHAPEL, Chapel Walk (SO 94622224), was built in 1842–4 for a Unitarian congregation formed in 1832 by Thomas Faber of Bath. Brick with ashlar front and slate roof, in Romanesque style by H.R. Abraham of London. Gabled front with four graduated round-arched upper windows, central entrance and flanking pilaster buttresses which formerly rose to a panelled upper stage with pyramidal finials but now reduced in height and gable cross removed.

Blake (1979) 25–6: CF (1871) 136–9: Evans (1897) 43–4.

CHIPPING CAMPDEN

(54) BAPTIST, High Street (SP 150392). Ashlar front and stone slate roof, built 1872. Entrance below gabled turret, windows with angular heads and stop-chamfered jambs.

(55) FRIENDS, Broad Campden (SP 15853795). When purchased by Quakers in 1664 this site was occupied by an orchard and a

building of two bays. The latter, which was used as a meeting-house, was enlarged to the S or possibly rebuilt in 1677 in which year Quarterly Meeting minutes of 29 March refer to assistance given to Friends at Campden 'in building their Meeting House'. Regular meetings ceased in 1874 and the building, which had been occasionally used by other denominations, was sold in 1931; it was repurchased in 1960 and has since been restored to its original use.

The meeting-house has stone walls and the roof is covered with local stone slates. The W front facing Meeting-house Lane has two windows of four lights with straight-chamfered mullions and moulded labels; to the S the round-arched doorway of late 18th-century character has plain imposts, keystone, and blind tympanum. The N and S ends are gabled and have stone copings and finials; in the S gable is a mullioned window of three lights with a moulded label, renewed or inserted in 1960. The E wall, of rough rubble, has two windows matching those in the opposite wall and to the S a plain doorway with timber lintel and 19th-century dormer window above.

The interior is of irregular shape (approx. $39\frac{3}{4}$ft by 16ft) and comprises a single large room and a wide passage to the S with gallery over having a panelled front with shutters above and below. Some 17th-century panelling remains at the N end behind the site of the stand. The roof is supported by three king-post trusses of the late 18th century; inside the N gable is the outline of an earlier coved plaster ceiling.

Gorman M.R., *Broad Campden Quakers* (1971): Sturge (1895) 15.

(56) Former WESLEYAN (SP 148390). Stone with ashlar E front and slate roof; built as a house in early 19th century, converted to a chapel c.1840 when the doorway was re-sited. Remains of defaced denominational inscription on N wall. (Restored to domestic use c.1975)

Cox, B.G., *Chapels and Meeting Houses in the Vale of Evesham* (1982) 10.

CHURCHAM

(57) WESLEYAN, Birdwood (SO 742187). Built c.1800 reputedly for the Countess of Huntingdon's Connexion and later sold for Methodist use. Brick and tile with broad N front of three bays with two tiers of wide round-arched windows, central entrance now altered and flush ashlar quoins at each end. Plain gabled end

walls with porch at E end added in late 19th century. School-room of similar date built against S side and early 19th-century cottage of two stories adjacent to west. Interior with E gallery, refitted in late 19th century.

CINDERFORD

(58) WESLEYAN (SO 658140). Stone and slate with gabled ashlar front having sharply stepped octagonal corner buttresses surmounted by tall thin pinnacles and an elaborate cross finial to the

gable. Central porch with shield-shaped tablet and decayed inscription 'WESLEY CHAPEL 1849'; five-light traceried window above.

CIRENCESTER

(59) GOSDITCH STREET CHAPEL (SP 022021). The origins of the Presbyterian society, in existence by the late 17th century, are obscure and although the curate, Alexander Gregory, was ejected

in 1662 there is no direct evidence that he formed a separate society. A licence for Presbyterian worship was applied for in 1672 and by 1690 John Beeby or Beebee, ejected vicar of Tideswell, Derbys., was pastor. The society, which by the 19th century had adopted Unitarian doctrines, was disbanded in 1980.

The site of the meeting-house behind other property on the SW side of the street appears to have been in use by the late 17th century and the building is of that period, although much altered internally in 1891. The walls are of rubble with a later rendering and the roof is hipped and tiled around a central valley. The SE wall has a wide round-arched doorway with a keystone bearing the false date 1648 and two mullioned windows of two lights all beneath a moulded cornice possibly of the early 19th century; to the left is a similar window with hinge-pins for external shutters, and five upper windows one of which has been inserted. The NW wall has four bays of windows to the lower stage, partly altered, and gallery windows at each end. In the SW wall are two former gallery windows of two lights and in the opposite wall is a small blocked doorway near one corner.

The interior (25¾ft by 46ft) has an original gallery at the NE end now altered to form an upper room, with a front of six bolection-moulded panels; a corresponding SW gallery was removed, the pulpit formerly against the NW wall re-sited at the SW end and the seating renewed in 1891.

Fittings – *Chair*: spirally turned legs and tall back with carved upper rail above two cane panels, 17th-century. *Clock*: on front of gallery, with shaped face and Chinese scene on pendulum case, signed John Cannon, with false date '1648', early 18th-century. *Communion Table*: oak, square, with turned legs and grooved rails, late 17th-century. *Monuments*: in burial-ground at rear, several table-tombs of mid 18th century and later. *Plate*: includes a two-handled cup of 1732.

Evans (1897) 50–1: Murch (1835) 25–34: *UHST* v (1931–4) 262–87, 329–30.

(60) BAPTIST, Coxwell Street (SP 02150215). Built 1856–7 for a church formed in the mid 17th century; gabled ashlar front with round-arched windows grouped over entrance.

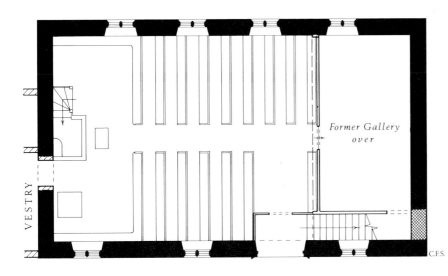

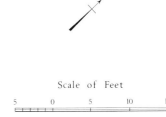

Gosditch Street Chapel
CIRENCESTER
Gloucestershire

N

Scale of Feet

5   0   5   10   15

VESTRY

Former Gallery over

C.F.S.

(61) Former STRICT BAPTIST, Park Street (SP 021021). Built 1854 for seceders from the earlier Baptist church, led by Joseph Tanner; closed c.1930. Pedimented ashlar front with two wide round-arched windows, now shortened and entrance between replaced by garage doors.

Oliver (1968) 113–14.

(62) FRIENDS, Thomas Street (SP 021022). Meetings were being held in or about Cirencester by 1660 in which year land at Siddington was acquired for a burial ground. In 1673 a lease of the present site was obtained and the earliest part of the existing structure is of this date. Some alterations were made to the building in 1726 and in 1809–11 a second meeting-house was built at the SW end. A porch with minor rooms was added against the NW wall in 1865. Regular meetings ceased in 1922 but were resumed in 1949.

The meeting-house stands on the SE side of the street; it has rubble walls and the roof is covered with stone slates. The NW front is partly obscured by a house and by the late 19th-century porch which has a round-arched doorway and windows below a boldly inscribed parapet. The SE side is of two distinct periods with dates 1673 and 1810 above the doorways, the earlier having a steeper roof-pitch; both parts have round-arched windows with hung sashes and intersecting glazing bars of the early 19th century.

SE side.

The interior (originally about 36ft by 27ft) is now largely of the early 19th century with a wide passage flanked by shutters formed out of one end of the original meeting-room separating the two parts of the building. The larger room to the NE has a stand with panelled front and back and two entrances with balustraded handrails; the ceiling is supported by four slender Doric columns inserted to strengthen the floor of an attic room which is approached from the adjacent house. The smaller meeting-room has a gallery at the SW end formerly balanced by another on the opposite wall.

Books: small library of early 18th-century Quaker books.
Stephens, L., *Cirencester Quakers, 1655–1973* (1973).

(63) Former WESLEYAN, Gloucester Street (SP 021024). Stone and slate with pedimental front gable and three round-arched windows above later porch. Built 1808, oval tablet removed; now Barton Hall Youth Centre.

COLEFORD

(64) BAPTIST (SO 574106). Built in 1858 by C.G. Searle for a church founded in 1799. Rubble with ashlar dressings and slate roofs.

(65) Former COUNTESS OF HUNTINGDON'S CONNEXION (SO 574106). Rendered rubble and hipped roof, greatly altered on conversion to a house 'Huntingdon House'. Built c.1788–90, closed c.1819, subsequently used by Wesleyans and as infants' school. Three-bay front formerly with rusticated quoins.

Bright (1954) 37–46.

(66) CONGREGATIONAL (SO 575109). Rendered walls and hipped slate roof, three-bay front with two tiers of round-arched windows with later frames and moulded cornice with name INDEPENDENT CHAPEL above projecting centre bay and date 1842 above central Doric-columned porch. Galleries added c.1854–5.

COWLEY

(67) Former STRICT BAPTIST, Birdlip (SO 927142). 'Moriah Chapel' of stone with gabled three-bay front is dated 1841 above the original entrance. Round-arched windows with later frames. Closed c.1954.

Oliver (1968) 112–13.

DEERHURST

(68) Former MORAVIAN, Apperley (SO 859276). Built in 1750 together with a small cottage alongside which served as the minister's house. In the early 19th century the property was leased and in 1845 sold to Wesleyans who in 1901 built a new chapel nearby and rebuilt the cottage. The former chapel (20ft by 30¼ft externally), now used for storage has brick walls and a tiled roof. The broad front is of three bays with a brick dentil eaves

cornice, flat-arched doorway and two segmental-arched windows; there are two similar windows in the rear wall.

Fittings – *Chair*: in present vestry, with panelled back and turned supports to arms, 17th-century. *Monuments*: include fragments of six late 18th-century Moravian tablets, five of which England records in a more complete state, (1) Elizabeth Heath, 1770; (2) Esther Hope [S.S.], 1771; (3) Timothy Watts, M.B., 1769; (4) William Dovey, M.B., 1768; (5) —— ——, W., 1778; (6) small fragment of taller stone, possibly James Garne, 1780.

England I (1886) 5 and pl.7.

DRYBROOK

(69) BAPTIST, Ruardean Hill (SO 638168). Gabled front with simple Venetian window; mid 19th-century.

DURSLEY

(70) CONGREGATIONAL, Parsonage Street (ST 754982). Meetings of Presbyterians or Independents were commenced about 1702 by the Rev. Joseph Twemlow of Cam Meeting and a meeting-house was built in Water Street *c.*1718. Preaching by George Whitefield in the mid 18th century resulted in the formation of a separate Calvinistic Methodist society in Dursley for which the first 'Tabernacle' was erected *c.*1760. The new cause flourished at the expense of the older meeting which eventually ceased and the meeting-house was for a time used as a school. The Presbyterian meeting-house on the W side of Water Street (ST 758981) is now a roofless shell with rubble walls partly

rendered at the front and traces of a blocked doorway to the left of the remaining round-arched entrance.

The present 'Tabernacle' (now URC) was built on a new site in 1808. The walls are of coursed stone with ashlar dressings. The SE end wall, which resembles Uley (154), has a pediment with inscribed trefoil panel above two pointed-arched windows; the lower stage is covered by a later porch. The SW side, of three bays with two tiers of similar windows with stone Y-tracery, has a pedimented centre bay in which was the original entrance. The interior was entirely refitted *c.*1880 and the entrance re-sited in the end wall.

Monuments: in chapel (1) John Dando 'hattmaker', 1775, and Susanna his widow, 1791; (2) Hannah Rudder, 1808, signed Daw; (3) John Trotman 'Card Board maker', 1839, and Ann his wife, 1836; (4) Rev. William Bennett, 1830; (5) William Smith, 1829; (6) Richard Trotman 'baker', 1810; (7) Isaac Danford, 1788, and Rachael his widow, 1802; (8) William King, 1803, signed J. Green and son, Gloucester.

Evans, D.E., *As Mad as a Hatter: Puritans and Whitfieldites in the History of Dursley and Cam* (1982): Montgomery, E.C., *Milestones . . .* (1958).

FAIRFORD

(71) Former BAPTIST, Milton Street (SP 149009). A Baptist church originated *c.*1700 at Meysey Hampton moving to Fairford in 1724, when a 'New built House lately erected in Fairford' was registered for worship. The meeting-house was much altered and refronted in 1853. An Independent church also

existed in the early 18th century, building a new meeting-house in 1744 which was replaced in 1862 by a small Gothic chapel, 'Croft Chapel', designed by T. Rogers Smith (demolished 1965). In 1919 the two societies formed a united church meeting in the Baptist chapel.

The chapel has stone walls and a hipped slate roof. The NW front of three bays has thin terminal pilasters, a moulded cornice and parapet with anthemion ornament at the corners, and the date MDCCCLIII on raised block at the centre. The SE wall retains traces of two lower windows and one above, all of early 18th-century date. The rear wall has two round-arched windows flanking the pulpit. A mid 19th-century Sunday-school adjoins to the north-west.

The interior (35ft by 30ft) was entirely refitted in the 19th century and has a single gallery opposite the pulpit. Some fielded panelling from former pews has been re-used as a dado around the walls.

Monuments: in chapel (1) Rev. Daniel Williams, 1841, 45 years pastor; (2) Rev. Thomas Davis, 1784, 40 years pastor, wooden tablet; in burial-ground in front of chapel, several large monuments and headstones of 18th century and later, including (3) William Thomson, 1779, with brass inscription plate.

CYB (1863) 344.

FALFIELD   *Avon*

(72) CONGREGATIONAL, Mount Pleasant (ST 682926). Built 1813, rebuilt 1843. Schoolroom to S, 1848.

FRAMPTON COTTERELL   *Avon*

(73) CONGREGATIONAL, Upper Chapel Lane (ST 672812). North of the present 'Zion Chapel' of 1873 (now URC and Methodist) is the former chapel built *c*.1800, a plain building with rendered walls and pantiled roof, much altered *c*.1840 and in recent years. *Monuments* in burial-ground include several table-tombs of the early 19th century.

FRAMPTON ON SEVERN

(74) CONGREGATIONAL (SO 747088). The chapel, standing on a concealed site behind buildings on the NW side of the green, is said to have been built in 1760; a lower Sunday-school wing was added alongside in 1849. The walls of the older portion are of brickwork above a plinth formed of dark blocks of copper slag; the roof is tiled and has a double ridge with central valley at collar level. The wing is of brick and slate. The double-gabled SW front has a central entrance with pointed-arched window above and a low annexe alongside incorporating a later gallery staircase. Two wider windows with wooden tracery in pointed-arched heads occupy the side walls, blocked against the school, and two windows at the NE end flank the pulpit.

The interior (33ft by 27ft) was partly refitted in the early 19th century and has a SW gallery of that period with a panelled and balustraded front supported by two cast-iron columns.

Fittings – Monuments: in chapel (1) Rev. William Richardson, 1847, and Elizabeth his wife, 1843, signed Felix Morgan, Frampton; (2) William Barnard, 1802, Elizabeth his widow, 1825, and William their son, 1783, signed Pearce; (3) Thomas King, 1783, and Sarah his widow, 1793, sarcophagus-shaped tablet above two draped urns, signed J. Pearce, Frampton; (4) John son of Thomas and Jane Wiles, 1786, oval tablet surmounted by standing figure, signed J. Pearce, Frampton; (5) Daniel Hewlett, builder, 1822, and his three wives Elizabeth, 1786, Ann, 1794, and Lydia, 1843; (6) George Barnard, 1815, Elizabeth his wife, 1809, and three children, signed E. Morgan, Frampton. *Seating*: box-pews with arched end panels, *c*.1840, and plain side benches with shaped supports and later backs.

GLOUCESTER

(75) BARTON STREET CHAPEL (SO 834184) was built in 1699 for a society of Presbyterians and Independents of which James Forbes, formerly lecturer in the Cathedral, was pastor. In 1715, three years after Forbes' death, the congregation divided, the Independents forming a separate church while the Presbyterians retained possession of the chapel to which they called ministers of

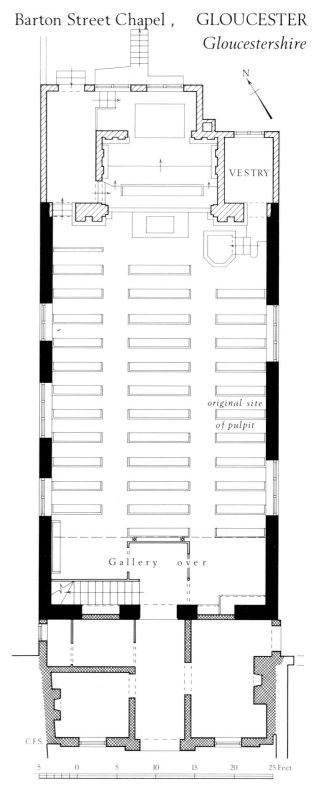

Barton Street Chapel, GLOUCESTER
Gloucestershire

VESTRY

original site of pulpit

Gallery over

C.F.S.

5   0   5   10   15   20   25 Feet

increasingly unorthodox views; by 1815 the society was commonly regarded as Unitarian.

The chapel is set back on the N side of the street behind the

Exterior from E.

Interior from SW before 1893, from a water-colour drawing in Gloucester Public Library.

(75) GLOUCESTER. Barton Street Chapel.

Floor slab to James Forbes, 1712.

line of other buildings and concealed by an extension of 1844. In 1893 the N end was rebuilt to provide an organ-chamber and vestry and the interior was refitted. In 1968 the building was derelict and the congregation met privately. (Since demolished)

The original building has brick walls and a hipped roof now covered with slate. Prior to 1844 the S front, concealed from the street by a brick boundary wall, had a central doorway and two upper and two lower windows which remain internally; the N wall was similarly fenestrated. The E wall has two wide segmental-arched windows which formerly flanked the pulpit. The W wall has three windows with original wood frames. The S front of 1844 is of ashlar with a pediment above two tiers of windows in three bays; a central entrance leads to a passage between minor rooms with a schoolroom above.

Before 1893 the interior of the chapel ($27\frac{1}{2}$ft by 49ft) had galleries at the N and S ends and a cross gallery to the W which was probably an addition; a central aisle between box-pews led to a doorway in the N wall giving access to a small burial-ground at the back. The pulpit was central against the E wall with a canopy over. In the refitting a small gallery was built at the S end and a short chancel for the choir with organ-chamber behind was added to the north. The original roof structure remains with three king-post trusses and radiating struts.

Fittings – *Communion Table*: Murch (1835) refers to 'a handsome communion table with a marble slab'; unlocated. *Library*: a considerable library left to the congregation by the Rev. James Forbes in 1712 was removed in 1715 by the Independents (see below).

Monuments and *Floorslabs*. *Monuments*: in chapel (1) John Dobbins, 1844; (2) William Tupsley Washbourne, 1842, timber merchant; (3) Lucy Ann Sharp, 1836; (4) Richard Chandler, 1810; (5) William Price, 1815; (6) Rev. Henry Davies Ll.D.,

1848, 12 years pastor; (7) William Washbourn, 1816 (monuments 2, 4, 6 are by Cooke, monument 1 is by W. Russell and 3 by George Sharpe, all of Gloucester). *Floorslabs*: (1) James Forbes A.M., 1712, with shield-of-arms, worn Latin inscription and later brass tablet, reset on W wall from vault in front of former pulpit; (2) Thomas Steel, 1752, Sarah his widow, 1775, and Elizabeth their daughter, 1782; (3) Elizabeth, wife of Nathaniel Washbourne, 1839.

Evans (1897) 94–5; Lloyd, W., *A Brief Account... of the Protestant Dissenting Meeting-house in Barton Street, Gloucester* (1899): Murch (1835) 4–18: *UHST* VI (1935–8) 383–4.

(76) CONGREGATIONAL, Southgate (SO 829183). A section of the Barton Street congregation seceded *c*.1715, retaining in their possession the library and communion plate (sold 1966 and 1923 respectively) of the parent society. A meeting-house was built in 1730 on the site of the parish church of St Owen, enlarged in 1830 and replaced by the present building in 1849–51. This is of stone with a slate roof, in the Decorated style with a gabled front having a tall five-light traceried window above the entrance; the sides are of five bays with aisles and cusped clerestory windows. (URC)

CHST X (1927–9) 100–4: Lander, T.J., *The History of Southgate Congregational Church, Gloucester, 1660–1972* (1972).

(77) FRIENDS, Greyfriars (SO 831183). The meeting-house of 1834–5 by Samuel Whitfield Dawkes, is of brick with stone dressings and a slate roof. The N front, formerly with a three-bay centre, now covered by a large entrance wing, has end bays with tall round-arched windows in arched recesses. The interior is divided into two rooms by a screen with hung shutters, the larger room to the E has an unusually high stand at the E end; that to the W has a raised seat against the S wall. At the entrance from the road is a *gatehouse* with segmental archway and blind panels above and at the sides; heightened and windows inserted.

GOTHERINGTON

(78) COUNTESS OF HUNTINGDON'S CONNEXION (SO 965296). Built 1833 on land given by the Hon. Henry Augustus Berkeley Craven.

GUITING POWER

(79) BAPTIST (SP 093249). Rubble and slate, gabled W front dated 1835. Original W gallery.

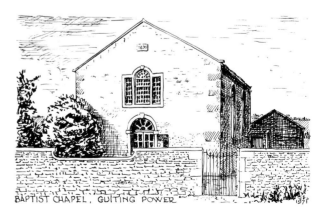

BAPTIST CHAPEL. GUITING POWER

HAMFALLOW

(80) WESLEYAN, Halmore (SO 699023). Brick with pointed-arched windows and wooden Y-tracery. Dated 1829

HAWKESBURY   *Avon*

(81) BAPTIST, Hillesley (ST 771897). The church formed about 1730 and reorganized in 1812 on Calvinistic principles, originally included both Particular and General Baptists. In 1732 the General Baptist Assembly sent a letter to encourage the church 'in their faithful ministry and good intentions of building a Meeting House' and this was registered in 1734. A link with the Seventh-day Baptists is also apparent in the appointment of William Hitchman of Natton as pastor in 1761 and in a donation received in 1766 for 'Sabbatarian Ministers' from the Mill Yard church in London. A vestry was added in 1770-1 and the chapel was rebuilt in 1823.

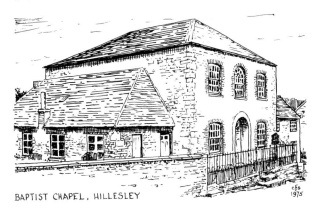

BAPTIST CHAPEL, HILLESLEY

The present building has rubble walls and a hipped slate roof. The S front is of three bays with two tiers of windows all with brick surrounds and segmental-arched heads except that above the central doorway which has a semicircular arch matching the entrance. Two windows in the N wall have round-arched heads of brick; the side walls are blank. A large vestry against the W side has a lean-to roof covered with stone slates.

The interior has an original gallery around three sides, now separated from the lower floor by an inserted ceiling, with contemporary box-pews and benches, some incorporating re-used 18th-century panelling. The lower seating and pulpit have been renewed.

Fittings – *Benefaction Board*: below W gallery, wood painted in imitation of marble, in moulded frame, recording bequests in 1794 and 1815 and a later inscription of 1846. *Monuments*: in chapel, a notable series of 18th-century wall monuments reset from the former meeting-house (1) Samuel Hook, 1768, and Margery his widow, 1775; (2) Joseph Bartlett, 1795, *et al.*; (3) Arthur Venn, 1768, and Arthur his son, 1794, with elaborate rococo cartouche and frame; (4) Mary (Venn) wife of John Taylor of Bristol, 1748, and William their son; (5–6) Edmund Dadge, 1768, and Hester his wife 1758, pair with swan-necked pediments and shaped cheeks; (7) Rev. Joseph Rodway, 1799, eight years assistant minister; (8) John Boulton of Killcott, 1795, reputedly a highwayman, with several cautionary texts, concluding 'All that's ever got by Thieveing Turns to Sorrow,

Shame, and Pain. Dr. Watts'; (9) William Rugg, 1794, and Thomas Davis, 1795; (10) Samuel Chappel, 1766, 'who died by the overturning of the Stage Coach at Faringdon, Berks.', and Ann his second wife, 1747.

Chappell K., *Hillesley Baptist Church, 1730–1980* [1980].

(82) CONGREGATIONAL, Hawkesbury Upton (ST 781869). 1844.

(83) PRIMITIVE METHODIST, Inglestone Common (ST 760884). 1836.

HAWLING

(84) WESLEYAN (SP 067231). Stone with hipped slate roof. Tablet dated 1837.

HEWELSFIELD

(85) Former CONGREGATIONAL (SO 567022). Opened 1822; derelict 1973.

(86) MORAVIAN, Brockweir (SO 540011). A new society was formed under Rev. Lewis West and the chapel built 1832–3 at the cost of the Bristol congregation. The chapel has rendered walls and a tiled roof with a bell-cote at the N end containing one bell; entrance in small porch at S and four lancet windows in each side wall. *Sunday-school* to E, of brick, by Foster and La Trobe of Bristol, late 19th-century.

Monuments: in burial-ground to W, flat marker-stones, also dwarf obelisk to Ann West, 1834, Zinzendorf Lewis West, 1839, and Louis Montgomery West, 1876.

England II (1887) 5.

KING'S STANLEY

(87) BAPTIST, Middleyard (SO 820032). Stone and tile, built 1824 for a church claiming to have originated in 1640. Gabled front with ball finials, two tiers of round-arched windows and later two-storied porch; blocked lunette in main gable. *Monuments*: in burial-ground, early 19th-century stones with brass inscription plates include (1) Rev. James Williams, 1818, signed Richard Dean, K[ing's] S[tanley], Engraver (plate 17in. by 12in.) (See p. 106).

(88) Former PRIMITIVE METHODIST, Selsley Road (SO 813034). Brick front with defaced tablet formerly dated 1861.

KINGSWOOD (near Bristol)   *Avon*

(89) BAPTIST, High Street, Hanham (ST 646722). A chapel built *c.*1721 for a church formed in 1714 and described as of stone with a parapet and round-headed windows has been demolished since 1965. Its successor of 1907 to the W, Gothic by La Trobe and Weston, has been drastically altered. *Monuments*: reset in vestibule of church hall, Charles Whittuck, 1788; in burial-ground, several headstones of late 18th century and after, some with winged cherub's heads, reset against E boundary.

Eayrs (1911) 149–153: Pevsner (1970) II, 260.

(90) WHITEFIELD'S TABERNACLE, Park Road (ST 649739). The spiritual needs of the colliers of Kingswood were an early concern of the Methodist preachers and a school-chapel was built in 1739 to which John Cennick was appointed as one of the two masters. In February 1741 after he had embraced Calvinistic

sentiments Cennick left with about fifty supporters and organized a separate society. In June of that year George Whitefield, who had encouraged the commencement of the former building but who had also subsequently revised his beliefs, wrote to Cennick from London with instructions to 'lay the foundations immediately' of the new Society Room at Kingswood, but to 'take care of building too large or too handsome'. The building was also used as a school-chapel, and in the disputes over its occupancy which followed Cennick's transfer of allegiance to the Moravians, in December 1745, it is referred to as 'Kingswood School'. It appears from the minutes of the English Calvinistic Methodist Association that Cennick and his supporters had retained possession of the building and that until the return of George Whitefield to London in 1748 the Calvinistic Methodists experienced difficulty in maintaining their rights. No further certain references to the building are known until after Whitefield's death in 1770, the first deed quoted being dated 1775 and followed by a trust deed of 1802. In the latter year a Sunday-school was commenced, meeting in the Tabernacle, and in 1830 further accommodation for this was provided alongside. In 1851 a new chapel was built nearby and placed in trust for Congregationalists to which denomination

the church by then adhered. (Now URC)

The *Tabernacle* stands behind other buildings on the N side of Regent Street, W of Park Road (formerly Tabernacle Lane). The walls are of rubble mostly covered by later rendering, and the roofs, in three sections parallel to the front, are hipped and covered with pantiles. The building dates from the mid 18th century and may incorporate parts of the Tabernacle of 1741. (Belden (p. 196) gives a date 1752 suggestive of a rebuilding comparable with that at the Moorfields Tabernacle in London, but no documentary support for this date has yet been found.)

The N front closely follows the design of the colliers' school-chapel of 1739 and is thus most likely to be part of the original structure. In the prototype the front was of five bays with a wide central doorway, wheel window above, flanking round-arched windows and minor entrances in the end bays with smaller windows over. At the Tabernacle the central doorway has been blocked and the upper window lengthened to match those in the adjacent bays, although the head remains higher. The minor entrances in the end bays have been moved nearer to the ends of the wall but small segmental-arched windows remain above the sites of the former doorways. The front corners of the wall have quoins of large blocks of cast purple slag, visible below the

Whitefield's Tabernacle, KINGSWOOD   *Gloucestershire*

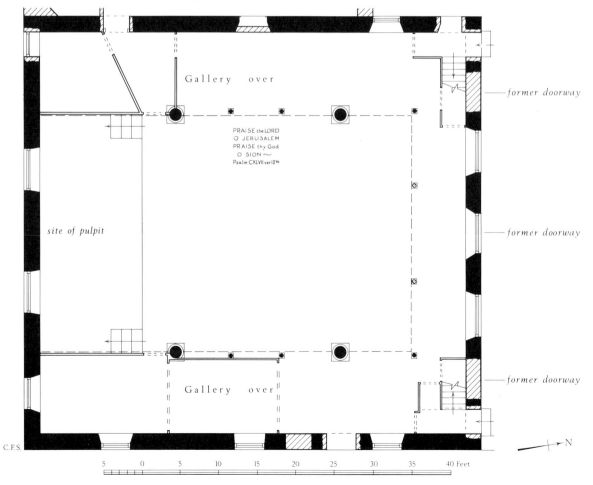

Gallery over

PRAISE the LORD
O JERUSALEM
PRAISE thy God
O SION ~
Psalm CXLVII ver 12th

site of pulpit

Gallery over

C.F.S.

former doorway

former doorway

former doorway

N

5   0   5   10   15   20   25   30   35   40 Feet

E side.

rendering at the NE corner; other pieces of this material are found elsewhere in the walling.

The S wall has a round-arched window each side of the pulpit and segmental-arched upper windows at the ends of the galleries. One original window remains below the E gallery but no trace of a corresponding window is visible; a modern opening has been made to the west. The E wall has three segmental-arched upper windows and three plain sash windows below; one doorway has been inserted and to the S is the site of another. The W wall, mostly covered by the 1830 Sunday-school block, was similar to the foregoing.

The interior (55ft by 50¼ft) is considerably larger than was the 1739 school-chapel, reputedly about 30ft by 60ft. There is a flat plaster ceiling without a cornice and the two principal valley-beams of the roof are supported by pairs of tall stone columns having attic bases on high square plinths and simple bell capitals with a single band of acanthus-leaf ornament. A gallery with fielded panelled front, perhaps dating at least in part from 1802, is carried around three sides supported by the principal columns and by slender intermediate shafts; the N gallery cuts across the line of the front windows. The gallery staircases in the NE and NW corners have been rebuilt and re-sited. The middle panel of the W gallery front is of stone, cut and painted to resemble the adjacent panels, and inscribed with a text from *Psalm* cxlvii.12. When the building was converted to Sunday-school use *c.*1851 a low platform was built at the S end to replace the pulpit and any original seating has also been removed.

The present *Chapel*, W of the former, was built in 1851 to the designs of Henry Masters of Bristol 'in the early English style'. The walls are of rubble with ashlar dressings and the roof is slate covered. The flanking towers of the S front were originally uniform; one has been reduced in height and a central tower has been removed. The interior comprises a nave and aisles of five bays with pointed-arched arcades on octagonal piers. At the N end is a polygonal apse for the organ and choir and at the opposite end is a small gallery for children which has external entrances and staircases in the front towers. The communion table, of wood in the form of a length of Gothic arcading, which formerly stood in front of a platform has been divided; this superseded the original intention of an open stone pulpit which would serve both purposes. The seating comprises open pews, with plain benches in the aisles to which backs have been added.

A large burial-ground between and to the N of the two buildings contains monuments of the 19th century and later.

Other fittings include – *Baptismal Basin*: white pottery bowl with grey marbled decoration, inscribed on two faces '*WHIT-FIELDS/TABERNACLE*', early 19th-century. *Sunday-school Banners*: two, with illustrations of the Tabernacle and its successor. (Demolition of 1851 chapel proposed 1981)

Belden [*c.*1930] 196–7: *Bristol Congregational Monthly* (May 1928): *CYB* (1851) 259: Eayrs (1911) 161–5, and *passim*: England I (1886) 11: *LRSP* XI (1975) 28–9, 38.

(91) WESLEYAN, Blackhorse Road (ST 645738). The colliers' school-chapel of 1739 (see above) continued to serve as a place of Methodist worship until 1843. It originally comprised a central room about 30ft square used for services and other purposes, and, at each end, two rooms to the ground floor and two above

which at first included some living accommodation, but in 1803 about when the colliers' school was discontinued the upper rooms were incorporated into the chapel and the lower rooms were combined. From 1748, when the Kingswood (Methodist) School was established, it was used additionally as the school chapel. After the removal of the boarding school to Bath the building was repaired in 1897 for use by a Reformatory school. It was demolished *c*.1917.

The present chapel, about ¼ mile NE of the former, was built in 1843 'largely by the efforts of Samuel Budgett' to serve the Wesleyan society, with seats reserved for the school. This has rendered walls and a slate roof. The N front has an open pediment, three conjoined round-arched windows above a central porch, and two side entrances. The side walls, of four bays, have tall arched upper windows and smaller openings below. The interior has an original gallery around three sides. The S end has been altered. Mid 19th-century box-pews remain throughout most of the chapel with some open-backed benches in the gallery.

Glass: in all windows, obscured plain glass with a narrow intermediate band following the outline of the opening. *Monuments*: in chapel (1) Samuel Budgett, 1851; (2) Edwin, son of Samuel and Ann Budgett, 1849.

Former 'Wesleyan School' of 1850 to S in similar style. (Congregation united with and removed to 'Zion Chapel', Two Mile Hill Road, Bristol (30), 1978; demolition of 1850 school proposed 1979)

Eayrs (1911) 49–59, 119–23, 183–4.

(92) FREE METHODIST, Chapel Road, Hanham (ST 643724). 'Founded 1851, enlarged 1903', with mid 19th-century pedi-

mented front of ashlar; apparently designed by D. Whitchurch. (Entirely refronted before 1981)

Eayrs (1911) 193.

(93) MORAVIAN, Regent Street (ST 649738). When John Cennick and his adherents were dispossessed of the Tabernacle *c*.1748 they removed to temporary premises, building a new chapel in 1756–7. This was a plain building with two round-arched windows and a gabled porch at one side and a two-storied minister's house attached to one end. The present chapel, of 1856–7, comprises a nave, transepts and a S apse. In the burial-ground are rectangular marker-stones of varied design dating from the 18th century.

Eayrs (1911) 178–81: England I (1886) 11.

KINGSWOOD (near Wotton-under-Edge)

(94) CONGREGATIONAL (ST 748920). 'A new built house at Kingswood', then a detached part of Wiltshire, was registered for use as a meeting-house in April 1702. This probably served the present church which was formed in the late 17th century apparently as a Presbyterian society. The chapel, 50 yards NE of the parish church, dates from the early 19th century and has walls of coursed stone rubble and a hipped roof now covered in patent tiles; a vestry along the N end has a lean-to roof of slate. The S front is of alternating deep and narrow stone courses. Two round-arched windows at the N end flank the pulpit. The roof is surmounted by a wooden bell-cote with one bell, a clock-face to

CONGREGATIONAL CHAPEL, KINGSWOOD, Nr Wotton

the W and a weather-cock above. Early 19th-century gallery around three sides with fielded panelled front; otherwise refitted.

Monuments: in burial-ground (1) Rev. Charles Daniell, [1832], 26 years pastor; (2) Rev. James Griffiths of Wotton-under-Edge, 1868; (3) Rev. William Davies, 18[?]7, 49 years minister; (4) Rev. William Coleman Woon, 1854, and William Harris his son, 1855.

LECHLADE

(95) BAPTIST, Sherborne Street (SU 214997). Built 1817. Pedimented front gable with lunette, round-arched doorway and two tiers of plain sash windows.

Before alteration.

LEONARD STANLEY

(96) WESLEYAN, The Street (SO 802035). Three-bay front with two tiers of sash windows. Opened 1809.

LITTLEDEAN

(97) CONGREGATIONAL, Broad Street (SO 670134). Built in 1820 for a congregation gathered about 1795 which from 1813 had met in a converted house. Rendered walls and hipped slate roof; segmental-arched doorway and shaped canopy between round-arched windows. Small burial-ground in front with early 19th-century monuments.

Bright (1954) 16–19.

(98) CONGREGATIONAL, Popes Hill (SO 687143). Dated 1844, much altered.

LONGNEY

(99) CONGREGATIONAL (SO 762127). Brick front; oval tablet dated 1839.

MANGOTSFIELD URBAN   *Avon*

(100) BAPTIST, Salisbury Road, Downend (ST 651765). The church, formed in 1814, owes its origin to Dr Caleb Evans, founder of the Bristol Education Society and pastor of the Broadmead church in Bristol, who in 1786 gathered a congregation and erected the chapel. After a period of neglect *c.*1873–93 the chapel was repaired and re-opened and the church re-formed; in 1903 the chapel was refitted and new vestries built. The adjacent Sunday-school was built in 1862.

The chapel is a tall building with rendered walls and a hipped roof. The front wall has a high parapet, stone quoins and rusticated surrounds to two round-arched upper windows; a later porch in a matching style has been rebuilt since 1974.

The interior (46ft by 30ft) has been much altered and a rear gallery removed. The original roof structure comprises four trusses each with a king-post, queen-posts and cross-bracing springing from the king-post at mid-height; on one of the queen-posts is the painted inscription 'Built 1786'.

Monuments: in chapel (1) Rev. Caleb Evans D.D., 1791, and Sarah (Hazle) his widow, 1817, grey and white marble with urn and swag in low relief; (2) Rev. John Foster, 1843, the essayist, pastor 1800–4 and 1817, erected 1896; (3) Rev. Joseph Mitchell, 1860 (*sic* but see below), 30 years pastor, and Ann his widow 1861; in burial-ground (4) John Foster, 1843, John his son, 1826, Sophia his daughter, 1868, and Elizabeth Peglar, 1877; (5) Rev. John Vernon, 1817, 'first pastor'; (6) Rev. Joseph Mitchell, 1859, *et al.*; (7) Rev. William Evans, 1892, 30 years pastor, *et al.*; (8) Thomas Nelmes, 1877, deacon, *et al.*, obelisk.

Eayrs (1911) 153–9.

MARSHFIELD   *Avon*

(101) THE OLD MEETING-HOUSE, High Street (ST 777737), was built in 1752 for a society of Independents and Presbyterians formed in the late 17th century; in 1672 John Fox, ejected vicar of Pucklechurch, was licensed here and in 1680 George Seal from Glamorgan is named as minister. An earlier meeting-house which appears to have been registered in 1699 stood on another site. In its later years the society favoured an heterodox ministry

and the cause died out in the mid 19th century. The building is now used for social purposes.

The meeting-house has walls of ashlar and a hipped roof covered with stone slates except at the front where it has been re-covered in patent tiles (remainder of roof tiled 1982). The walls

THE OLD MEETING-HOUSE, MARSHFIELD

have a stone plinth and a continuous platband linking the windows at impost height. The N front has rusticated quoins, a central segmental-arched doorway with rusticated surround and two round-arched windows with keystones; in the S wall are two similar windows, and in the E and W walls are gallery windows at a higher level. A tablet on the front wall is dated 1752.

The interior (25ft by 36¼ft) has a flat plaster ceiling with coved moulded cornice and an original central ceiling-rose. E and W galleries have fielded panelled fronts without intermediate supports. The N wall and the end walls at gallery level are divided into three bays by arcading. The lower walls have a dado of two tiers of reset fielded panelling from former pews and the site of the pulpit against the S wall is marked by an iron hand which served to support a canopy. In front of the meeting-house is a small forecourt and stone gate-piers.

Monument: in burial-ground to the S, 18th-century table-tomb with panelled sides and shaped corners. Reset as paving are fragments of other monuments. (Murch records monuments in the meeting-house to Rev. Evan Thomas, 1762, and Rev. David Evans, 1817, also a foundation stone of 16 October 1752 with a lengthy oecumenical inscription.) *Sundial*: on S wall, with Roman numerals and iron gnomon.

Murch (1835) 36–46.

MINCHINHAMPTON

(102) WESLEYAN, Littleworth (SO 849016). Built 1790 but much altered and refitted 1887. Rubble walls and hipped slate roof. Three-bay front with two tiers of round-arched windows and later entablature; four-bay sides with two rows of lancet windows except where later building adjoins. The interior (34½ft by 32½ft) has a gallery around three sides, refronted and repewed in 1887.

MITCHELDEAN

(103) CONGREGATIONAL (SO 664182). The church originated in the late 17th century, rebuilding its meeting-house in 1735 and 1798 and replacing it by the present chapel in 1822. The walls are

of rendered rubble and the roof is hipped and slated. The front entrance, inside an altered porch, has a round-arched head with keystone and above it is a simple Venetian window; two slightly pointed-arched windows in each side wall have intersecting glazing bars. The interior, largely refitted, has a back gallery. In the small burial-ground is a monument to Hester Partridge, 1784, daughter of Thomas and Mary Partridge, and Samuel their son, 1799.

Bright (1954) 2, 14–15.

MORETON-IN-MARSH

(104) CONGREGATIONAL, Oxford Street (SP 205325). Built 1860–1 in 'the Italian style' by Poulton and Woodman of

Reading, for a church formed in 1801. Stone and slate, with grouped round-arched windows. *Pitch-pipe*: early 19th-century.

CYB (1861) 281–4.

NAILSWORTH

(105) BAPTIST (ST 847995). Seceders from Forest Green Chapel *c*.1705 built a meeting-house at Shortwood in 1714–15 which was rebuilt in 1837. 'Shortwood Chapel', built on a new site in 1881, has an ashlar front of three bays with pilasters and a pediment into which the centre bay rises as an arch.

Ivimey IV (1830) 469–80: Thompson-Smythe, F., *Chronicles of Shortwood* (1916).

(106) CONGREGATIONAL, Spring Hill (ST 847999). The Independent meeting at Forest Green originated in the late 17th century, one of the first promotors being William Tray, ejected rector of Oddington. A meeting-house built *c*.1687 was enlarged to the front in the early 18th century, a large vestry added 1745, and a plaster ceiling constructed in the chapel in 1761. In 1821 a majority of the church erected the present 'Forest Green Chapel' on a new site. This has stone walls and a slate roof. The front of three bays with a wide round-arched doorway and two tiers of windows all with round-arched heads has a pedimented gable, rebuilt at the apex, with a large lunette inscribed with the date of erection. The interior which has a gallery around three sides was refitted *c*.1880 and later.

Russell, C., *A Brief History of the Independent Church at Forest Green, Nailsworth* (1912).

(107) FRIENDS, Chestnut Hill (ST 848995). Considerable support for Quaker teaching is known to have existed by 1655 and the present building may have been in use before 1689 when it was registered as a meeting-house. Some external repairs were carried out in 1794–5 and alterations were made to the interior in 1807 and 1819. The building, which stands at right angles to a slightly earlier house facing a courtyard, dates in part from the

(107) NAILSWORTH. Friends' meeting-house.

mid 17th century; the walls are of coursed rubble and the roof which is double with a central valley is covered with stone slates.

The W front has a wide round-arched doorway with keystone and imposts below a square label with diamond stops; to the right is a window formerly of four lights with a transome, now altered, and to the left is a smaller window of two lights and another above; the lower windows have moulded labels. The S end has two gables: below that to the E is a mullioned window of three lights with a moulded label, reduced in width and with a hung sash inserted in the early 19th century, and an upper window of two lights; below the other gable is the blocking of a lower window with timber lintel. The N wall, partly covered by the house, has windows below the E gable corresponding to those at the opposite end but variously altered.

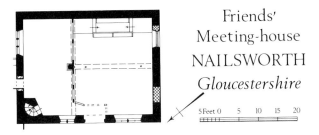

Friends'
Meeting-house
NAILSWORTH
Gloucestershire

5 Feet 0   5   10   15   20

The interior (24¼ft by 33¼ft) is unevenly divided into two rooms by an early 19th-century screen with shutters incorporating a substantial earlier post which supports one end of the valley beam above the principal room. The S room, much altered in the early 19th century, has a panelled dado and stand at the E end; the upper window in the S wall, formerly lighting an attic, has been altered to serve the room below. The N room has a stone spiral staircase in one corner leading to an upper room at this end.

Inscriptions: scratched on window cill of upper room, initials and dates including 1683, 1684. *Seating*: in upper room, crude open-backed benches with shaped oversailing ends and thin splayed legs, possibly 17th-century with backs added; in meeting-room, early 19th-century benches. The burial-ground for this meeting is at Shortwood.

NAUNTON

(108) BAPTIST (SP 114234). Built 1850. Stone and slate, gabled W end with porch between staircase wings; four-bay sides with pointed windows and stone Y-tracery. *Gates*: contemporary cast-iron gates next to road. *Monument*: in chapel, Robert Rowlands, 1851, and Hannah his widow, 1874, 'the only members who assisted in building the old chapel about the year 1798 that lived to see the new one opened for public worship in 1850'.

NEWENT

(109) CONGREGATIONAL, Broad Street (SO 721259). Built *c*.1844. Ashlar front with red brick sides and slate roof. Gabled front with traceried windows and ogee labels; cast-iron window frames. (URC)

NEWNHAM

(110) Former CONGREGATIONAL, Littledean Road (SO 690118). Rendered front of three bays with two tiers of round-arched windows. Built 1826; new chapel built nearby after 1859.

(109) NEWENT. Congregational chapel.

NORTHLEACH WITH EASTINGTON

(111) CONGREGATIONAL, Northleach (SP 113147). By T. Roger Smith, 1860. Gabled front with bell-cote. The open single-span

roof incorporates clerestory lighting to overcome the absence of side windows on a restricted site. (Closed before 1981)
CYB (1859) 256; (1861) 280, 282.

NORTON

(112) Former WESLEYAN, Bishop's Norton (SO 850245). Brick with hipped slate roof, triple-arched front with later porch and tablet dated 1841.

OLDBURY-UPON-SEVERN *Avon*

(113) WESLEYAN (ST 610925). Opened 1835; pantiled roof.

OLDLAND *Avon*

(114) Former WESLEYAN, Longwell Green (ST 659711). Three-bay gabled front with later porch. Opened 1823; transferred to Free Methodists *c.*1870.

(115) Former FREE METHODIST, Longwell Green (ST 659710). Three-bay front with worn tablet dated ?1853. Used as Sunday-school after *c.*1870.

Eayrs (1911) 193, 235.

(116) WESLEYAN, Warmley Tower (ST 669725). Rendered front with two tiers of windows. Dated 1833.

OLVESTON *Avon*

(117) Former FRIENDS, The Green (ST 601868). A meeting in Olveston was settled by *c.*1655 with Walter Clement as a principal supporter. The present building of 17th-century date was given to the society in 1696; in 1779 it was reported to be 'in a ruinous condition' and it was repaired in 1782 at a cost of £189 6s. 11d. The meeting-house was closed in 1872 and has since been converted to a private house.

The walls are of rubble and the roofs are pantiled. The W front has a wide doorway with ovolo-moulded frame between two windows of four lights with oak mullions; two gables have recently been added. The roof over the E half is in two parallel sections with half-hips to the rear and formerly with a lower roof between. The interior ($35\frac{1}{2}$ft by $32\frac{1}{2}$ft) is divided by partitions with shutters into a single meeting-room to the E with stand at the S end and two smaller rooms to the W with a room above which has two sashes opening to the principal room.

To the N is a former stable, square with hipped roof, in similar materials.

(118) WESLEYAN (ST 601872). Oval tablet dated 1820 in shaped gable.

PAINSWICK

(119) Former BAPTIST, Jack's Green, Sheepscombe (SO 889099). Broad three-bay front with pointed-arched windows. Built 1820 and sold to Primitive Methodists 1831 on removal to (123).

(120) CONGREGATIONAL, Gloucester Street (SO 867099). Independents, believed to have been active here from the mid 17th century, were supported in 1672 by Francis Harris, ejected curate of Deerhurst. In 1689 the Town Hall was registered for meetings, possibly by this society, and in 1705 a meeting-house was built which was recorded as Presbyterian. The present chapel was erected in 1803 largely through the efforts of the pastor the Rev. Cornelius Winter and drastically altered in 1892 to the designs of J. Fletcher Trew when it was named 'The Cornelius Winter Memorial Chapel'. (now URC)

This is a square stone building with hipped roof having two tiers of windows and a platband; two tall round-arched windows in the NE wall mark the former site of the pulpit. In 1892 a moulded cornice and parapet were added, many of the windows were altered or embellished and a porch built against the SW front. The interior, which had a gallery around three sides, was divided to provide an entrance lobby with staircase and vestry and an upper room at the front and a smaller chapel behind in which the pulpit was re-sited at the SE end facing a single gallery. SE of the chapel is a separate schoolroom dated 1844.

Glass: In SE window above pulpit, two angels with harps and vine-scroll border, by William Morris & Co., 1897–8. *Monuments*: in chapel (1) William Cox, 1866, clothier, and Henrietta (Wane) his wife, 1849, signed J. Wall, Stroud; (2) John Haynes, 1856, surgeon, and Harriet (Wane) his widow, signed C. Lewis, Cheltenham; (3) William Fowles, 1832, Elizabeth his widow, 1848, and Eliza their daughter, 1830; (4) Rev. Cornelius Winter, 1808, nearly twenty years pastor 'by whose Benevolence and exertions this Edifice was erected', and Miriam his widow, 1817; (5) Elizabeth Shepherd, 1805 and Martha Tyler, 1818, signed J. Pearce, Frampton; in vestibule (6) William West, 1792, 'Clerk of this Chapel'; (7) Sarah Thomas, 1839, and Joseph Beavins her son, 1861. Also, in chapel, a series of small late 19th-century memorials to 18th- and 19th-century pastors.

CYB (1893) 194–5.

(121) CONGREGATIONAL, Edge (SO 851097). Three-bay ashlar front with pediment and pilasters; built 1856 for a society formed by Cornelius Winter. Inside are open-backed benches and two box-pews flanking the entrance. The original pulpit (now removed) came from the church of St Mary le Crypt, Gloucester, where George Whitefield preached his first sermon. *Inscription*: slate tablet, loose outside, inscribed 'CONGREGATIONAL CHURCH TRUST 1856'. (Disused)

CYB (1857) 235.

(122) FRIENDS, Vicarage Street (SO 870097). Built in 1705–6 for an existing meeting which since 1658 had the use of a burial-ground at Dell Farm, the gift of Thomas Loveday. Major repairs

or alterations were made to the meeting-house in 1793–4; it was closed in 1894 and re-opened by Friends 1952. The walls are of squared stone with chimney-stacks on the E and W gables; the roof has been re-covered with blue slates. The S front has a central doorway, now blocked, with cambered stone lintel dated

Friends'
Meeting-house
PAINSWICK
Gloucestershire

5 Feet 0   5   10   15   20

C.F.S.

1706; to each side is a tall window with later timber lintel and hung sashes. In the E wall is a similar doorway below a gabled hood supported by shaped wooden brackets and two windows high in the gable. The W wall has two similar gable windows and a blocked window below.

The interior ($29\frac{3}{4}$ft by $23\frac{1}{2}$ft) comprises a single room with stand at the W end and small lobby to the E with shutters to the main room and a staircase leading to the upper floor. The staircase dates from the late 18th century and the attic floor, which provided residential accommodation, was largely refitted at that period. *Seating*: early 19th-century open-backed benches; front of stand removed.

Burial-ground: (SO 876094) N of Dell Farm, stone boundary-walls and W entrance closed by re-used stone slab with cast-iron plate dated 1658. Eight ledger stones, two with coffin-shaped outline, one with brass indent, with decayed inscriptions of 17th and 18th century to Loveday family.

(123) Former WESLEYAN, New Street (SO 867097). Built 1806, sold to Baptists 1831. Gabled front of three bays with two tiers of windows. Two tablets in gable inscribed with dates of erection and transfer.

(124) Former PRIMITIVE METHODIST, Bisley Street (SO 868097). 'Ebenezer Chapel' was built 1854 for a society formerly meeting in Vicarage Street.

PRESTBURY

(125) CONGREGATIONAL (SO 970238). Polychrome brick, corner tower with pyramid roof, 1865.

RANDWICK

(126) WESLEYAN (SO 831067). 'Randwick Chapel, Built 1807, Rebuilt 1824' is a substantial building of stone with a slate roof. The S end has a pedimental gable with inscribed tablet and bell-cote with one bell; two windows of three lights have pointed-arched heads and intersecting stone tracery. Long side-walls each with two pointed windows, and Sunday-school at N end. Refitted in late 19th century.

RODBOROUGH

(127) PRIMITIVE METHODIST, Butter Row (SO 856041). 'Zion Chapel' dated 1856.

For Rodborough Tabernacle see (140).

RUARDEAN

(128) BIBLE CHRISTIAN, Crooked End (SO 628176). Opened 1855.

RUSPIDGE

(129) BIBLE CHRISTIAN, Ruspidge (SO 651116). Squared stone front and rubble sides, each with two windows.

(130) BIBLE CHRISTIAN, Upper Soudley (SO 661103). Three-centred arched entrance and two small round-arched gallery windows. Tablet over doorway inscribed 'ZION CHAPEL 1846'.

SISTON

(131) FREE METHODIST, Bridgeyate (ST 682733). 'Ebenezer Chapel' dated 1810. Broad three-bay front extended at end in two stories.

SLIMBRIDGE

(132) Former CONGREGATIONAL, Cambridge (SO 746033). 'Union Chapel', built 1807, extended to rear 1876.

SODBURY   *Avon*

(133) Former BAPTIST, Hounds Road, Chipping Sodbury (ST 728821). 'REBUILT 1819'. Interior subdivided and floored for Sunday-school 1971.

STOW-ON-THE-WOLD

(134) BAPTIST, Sheep Street (SP 192256). The church originated as part of that at Moreton-in-Marsh, in existence by 1655, which came to be described as meeting near Moreton and Stow. The first known meeting-house at Stow was referred to as 'lately erected' in a lease of 18 April 1700 where its size is given as 37ft by 21ft with a burial-ground on the S side 51ft by 25ft with access from Back Street (now Sheep Street).

The present chapel built in 1852 on the site of the former, stands behind houses on the S side of the street and is approached through an arched passage of that period. The walls are of coursed rubble with ashlar dressings and the roof is hipped at a low pitch and covered with slates; wide, boarded, eaves are supported by paired brackets. The interior, refitted in 1892, has a N gallery only.

Fittings – *Book*: Geneva Bible with Apocrypha, 'printed at London by the deputies of Christopher Barker', 1597.

Bootscrapers: at N doorway, wrought-iron with scrolled standards, *c*.1852. *Inscription*: on stone reset in wall of outhouse, TB 1732. *Monuments*: in burial-ground (1) John Ellis, 1711; (2) Elizabeth Marsh, 1712; (3) John Marsh, 1700. *Plate*: includes two small tankards of 1709 given by Mrs Margaret Freeman of Guiting.

Blackaby, F.E., *Past and Present, History of the Baptist Church. Stow-on-the-Wold* (1892): Ivimey II (1814) 161–2: Oliver (1968) 115–16.

(135) Former FRIENDS (SP 193259). A meeting-house built in 1719 on a piece of land 47ft by 19ft, acquired in that year, stands in a lane behind the White Hart Hotel. The building, sold in 1887 and now used as a youth hostel, has rubble walls and a tiled roof. It has been much altered but blockings of former windows are visible in the end walls. The interior ($26\frac{1}{4}$ft by $17\frac{1}{2}$ft) has no old features.

Sturge (1895) 14.

(136) WESLEYAN, Sheep Street (SP 192257). Brick and stone with corner tower, built 1865; tablet dated 1814 reset from former chapel.

STROUD

(137) BAPTIST, John Street (SO 852051). Ashlar front of three bays with round-arched windows. Built 1824; much altered inside 1975.

(138) THE OLD CHAPEL, Chapel Street (SO 857051). The congregation formerly meeting here appears to have met in the late 17th century in Robert Viner's barn at Stroud Water which was registered in June 1689. The present site was acquired in 1704 and a meeting-house had been erected by 1711. Although the building was held in trust for Presbyterians, the church included Independents and by 1811, when John Burder was appointed pastor to revive the declining fortunes of the society, the cause had come to be regarded as Congregational. Burder's pastorate (1811–37) was marked by the first enlargement of the meeting-house to the S in 1813, and the flourishing condition in which he left the church was evinced by a further considerable alteration, heightening and refronting of the building in 1844; a detached

schoolroom was built to the N in 1854 and the chapel was largely refitted *c*.1881.

The walls are of rubble, rendered on the E side, and the roof is hipped and slated with a lead flat at the centre. The E and W walls of the early 18th-century structure remain and part of the N wall; the latter was pierced *c*.1844 when an organ chamber was added which has two round-arched windows on the N side. The W wall has two tiers of round-arched windows refashioned in 1844 but of which two to each level probably occupy the sites of the original openings; a ragged joint in the masonry marks the line of rebuilding to the south. The E wall is similarly fenestrated; the rendering was carried out prior to the heightening which is marked by a change in colour. The S front, added to

S front.

Exterior from NE.

provide a vestibule and staircases outside the former end of the building, is in the Romanesque style with two doorways and low staircase wings at the sides.

The interior (originally about 30ft by 40¼ft; enlarged to 45½ft by 40¼ft exclusive of the vestibule) has a plaster ceiling coved on all sides and a large semicircular arch at the N end opening to the organ chamber. The gallery, around three sides supported by wooden columns, was rebuilt or refronted in 1844. The S front, of 1813 and now internal, has a central entrance now blocked and replaced by two doorways.

Fittings – *Benefaction Boards*: in S vestibule, two, painted wood with shaped tops and leaf finials, recording eight benefactions, 1830–87, including a Communion service given 1830 by William and Ann Leach, and £1,300 given for renovation in 1881 by Mrs Franklin in whose memory a stained-glass window was erected on the E side of the chapel. *Monuments*: in vestibule (1) Henry Wyatt, 1847, Hannah his wife, 1826, and Priscilla his widow, 1865, double-arched Romanesque panel with shield-of-arms; (2) Elizabeth (Brownson) wife of John Grime, 1756; (3) Rev. John Burder M.A., 1867, 26 years pastor, with shield-of-arms; (4) Thomas Harmer, 1825, servant to Rev. John Burder, and Mary his widow, 1832; (5) Rev. William Harries, 1830, 28 years pastor; in chapel (6) Robert Morgan, 1740; (7) Richard Rawlin, 1725, Thomas Jenkins, 1749, and Samuel Ball, 1779, pastors, erected 1823; (8) Joseph Franklin, 1855, 'many years architect to the Corporation of Liverpool', Benjamin his brother, 1862, and Maria widow of the last, 1881, signed Hamlett, Stroud; (9) Mrs Susannah Davis, 1836, signed Hamlett; (10) John Okey, 1783, and Ann his widow, 1792; (11) Edward Okey, 1798, card-maker, Martha his widow, 1819, and three infants; (12) Anthony Paine, mercer, 1775, Sarah his widow, 1801, *et al*.; (13) Anthony Paine, clothier, 1735, Mary his widow, 1759, and Susannah their daughter 1760; (14) John Viner, 1723, and Sarah his sister, 1723; (15) Daniel Bloxsome, mercer, 1808, Sarah (Morley) his wife 1781, Ursula (Aldridge) his widow, 1828, and Sarah Aldridge her sister, 1811; externally, on E wall and adjacent are several reset 18th-century monuments, also brass tablets including (16) John Clissold, 1823, 'sexton of this Place 30 Years', *et al*.; further brass inscription plates on paving of E courtyard; in burial-ground N of chapel numerous monuments

In Memory of Henry Okey Clerk of y^s Church 41 Years, who died 3^d Jan: 1765; Æ: 67

of the 18th century and later including (17) Henry Okey, 1765, clerk, with inscription on brass tablet.

(Church united with Bedford Street 1970; chapel demolished 1977. The benefaction-boards and some of the monuments have been removed to Stroud Museum)

Fisher, P.H., *Notes and Recollections of Stroud, Gloucestershire* (1871) 319–28.

(139) CONGREGATIONAL, Bedford Street (SO 851052). A new congregation formed to relieve overcrowding at the Old Chapel built 'Bedford Street Chapel', originally named 'Union Chapel', in 1835–7. The names of Charles Barker and Dawkes (possibly Samuel Whitfield Dawkes) appear in the accounts against payments for plans. The chapel has walls of rubble faced at the front with ashlar. The front wall has a plain lower stage above which four fluted Ionic columns support a pediment; in the wide central bay is a Venetian window. The entrance is in a circular

stair tower to one side, in two stages surmounted by a dome and a (rebuilt) lantern. The body of the chapel has plain sides rounded to the rear with tall round-arched windows to the principal stage.

The interior of the chapel, which stands above Sunday-school rooms at ground level, is approached by a circular staircase. An original rear gallery was extended along the sides and around the apsidal end in 1851, and the three windows in the apse were blocked internally. The other windows were reglazed in 1889; alterations were made to the pews c.1919. The original pulpit, partly concealed by a platform, is circular and has a ring of Corinthian columns to the upper stage.

Fisher, *op. cit.*, 319–28: Nott, R., *The Bedford Street Congregational Church, Stroud* (1937).

(140) RODBOROUGH TABERNACLE (SO 846040). A preaching-house built in 1750 for a group of Calvinistic Methodist societies in the neighbourhood of Rodborough forms the nucleus of the present chapel. These societies founded by George Whitefield, together with others more remote, later became known as the 'Rodborough Connexion' and eventually adopted Congregational practices. The building (now URC), which has stone walls and a hipped slate roof, was enlarged to the W and heightened in 1837 and subsequently extended to the E by the addition of a Sunday-school. The earliest part (40¼ft by 42½ft externally) faces N and is of three bays with a central segmental-arched doorway, now reduced in width, between two windows with segmental-arched heads and keystones. Three upper windows have had round arches added when the wall was heightened. The extensions to E and W are each of two bays with matching windows. The main entrance is now at the W end set between two late 19th-century staircase pavilions which front the end wall of 1837 in which is a plain Venetian window.

The interior (now 58¾ft by 38½ft) was refitted in 1837 when

the pulpit was resited at the E end and a gallery with fielded panelled front built around four sides. The seating and pulpit are of later date.

Fittings – *Book*: in locked case, The Great Bible or 'Treacle Bible', mid 16th-century. *Chair*: high-backed with arms and open round splat back, called 'Whitefield's chair', 18th-century. *Monuments*: in chapel (1) Henry Hodges 1838, Hester his wife, 1831, and Rebecca his sister, 1874; (2) Samuel Marling, 1777 (also a brass), Hester his widow, wife of John Figgins, 1801 (also a brass), William Marling, 1859, and Sarah his wife, 1856; (3) Edward Dicks, 1832, and Elizabeth his wife, 1815; (4) Thomas Adams, 1770, first pastor, Elizabeth his first wife, 1765, and Hannah his second wife, 1800; (5) Rev. Robert Heath, 1800, and Benjamin his son, 1797; (6) Rev. Orlando Augustus Jeary, 1817, Sarah his wife, 1806, and Elizabeth his widow, 1822; (7) Anne, wife of Rev. Eliezer Jones, 1837, and their two children Mary Jane, 1835, and Louisa Anne, 1837. *Paintings*: in vestry, oil portraits of John Cennick and various ministers including Thomas Adams and John Rees (pastor 1813–23). *Miscellaneous*: Walking stick of George Whitefield and cane of Thomas Adams.

(141) EBLEY CHAPEL (SO 827049), the successor to a chapel of 1797 built for an Independent congregation which was for a

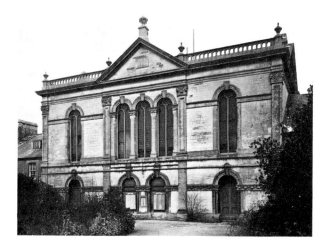

time associated with the Countess of Huntingdon's Connexion, was built in 1880–1 to designs of Rev. Thomas Thomas. It is a large building of stone having a wide S front with pedimented centre and wings with balustraded parapets and urn finials. The back is polygonal externally with a semicircular gallery facing the pulpit which is set between the front entrances. The manse adjacent to the W was built in 1798 with a room added in 1845; a cottage to the E is also of the late 18th century. (Demolished *c*.1972)

Criddle, L., *The Story of Ebley Chapel* [*c*.1947].

(142) Former METHODIST, Acre Street (SO 85450515). A society which had earlier suffered from internal dissentions had sufficiently recovered by 1763 to build what is now the oldest surviving octagonal Methodist chapel; John Wesley preached 'in the new house' on 18 March 1765 to an overflowing congregation. The building was greatly enlarged in 1796 by extension to the NW and superseded a century later by a new Wesleyan

Former Methodist Preaching - house, Acre Street STROUD *Gloucestershire*

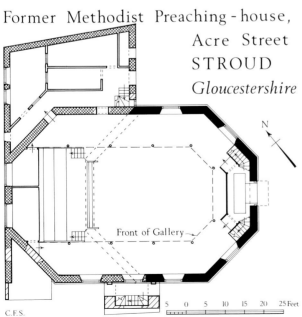

chapel in Castle Street, in the Classical style by James Tait of Leicester, opened 27 October 1876, closed 1981. The octagon is now used as the Salvation Army Citadel.

The former preaching-house has stone walls and a hipped slate roof. It was originally a regular octagon, the extension being accomplished by doubling the length of the sides and rebuilding one end. The original walls have a stone plinth, a flat-arched window to the lower stage and a smaller window above which terminated level with the eaves. The front doorway has a flat wooden canopy supported by shaped brackets. The walls of the extension are similarly fenestrated but with two large round-arched windows in the NW wall which formerly flanked the pulpit. A two-storied wing to the N may be contemporary with the enlargement. Alterations of 19th-century date included the erection of a short buttressing wing to the SW with wide flank walls enclosing raking timber shores and a narrow additional staircase between to the gallery. Pointed-arched heads in dormers were also added to the upper windows of the original building, the window over the entrance was blocked and a tall rendered parapet constructed at the front. The external character has also been much affected by the substitution of window frames with large panes in place of the original sashes. The interior (61ft by 40ft) has a gallery around five sides supported by timber columns with Roman Doric capitals. A large stepped platform has been constructed at the NW end with small rooms below and the principal windows at this end have been blocked. The roof was reconstructed after a fire in the early 20th century and the ceiling rebuilt at a slightly higher level.

(143) Former PRIMITIVE METHODIST, Parliament Street (SO 857052). Dated 1836. Now the Playhouse.

TETBURY

(144) BAPTIST, Church Street (ST 890931). A Particular Baptist church which claims to have been formed in 1721 appears to have occupied this site since 1764 if not earlier, a conveyance of 1719 refers to a building called The Red Lion which also appears in later documents and an inn called The Three Cups. A 'new built house in Tetbury' was registered for Baptist use in 1725. Two confronting buildings now stand within the boundary of the property: the present chapel and an earlier building which is supposed to have been its predecessor.

The earlier building, of rubble with a stone slate roof, has two gables to the front in each of which is a small attic window. Larger windows have been inserted below with round-arched heads of brick and keystones and a doorway of similar date and style between. Above the entrance a small window has been blocked and there are further signs of alterations elsewhere in the building. The interior which is narrow has been altered, probably by the removal of a floor, and now has a single end gallery with attics above.

The present chapel, of stone with a hipped stone slate roof, may be as late as *c*.1800. The front has two doorways and three upper windows all with round-arched stone heads with keystones. The interior, partly refitted, has an L-shaped gallery.

TEWKESBURY

(145) THE OLD BAPTIST CHAPEL, Church Street (SO 890325). A Particular Baptist church was in existence in Tewkesbury by 1655 in which year it was represented at the first meetings of an association of Midland Baptist churches. Although the first deed of the property in Old Chapel Court (formerly Millington's Alley and previously Merrie Cheaps or Millicheape's Alley) is dated 1620, being a conveyance from Edward Millicheape to Thomas Harris, carpenter, no specific reference to a meeting-house appears until 1711. No licences for Baptist meetings were issued under the 1672 Indulgence and the earliest monuments in the burial-ground date from c.1680. A reference in the parochial burial register (Matthews (1924) 214) to Paul Frewen, ejected vicar of Kempley, Glos., later Baptist minister at Trowbridge and Warwick, as 'speaker in ye Diss Bur Place' at Tewkesbury could indicate that some meetings were being held in the open. As a deed of 1686 mentions only a 'messuage divided into several tenements in Millington's Alley' the formal conversion of part or all of the property to a meeting-house may have been delayed until after Toleration in 1689. Further alterations to the building seem to have occurred in the late 18th century, but the need for a more convenient place of worship was eventually felt: the church books record 'Our meeting house being very old and much out of repair and not sufficient to accommodate the Congregation a purchase of ground was made in Barton Street and a new Meeting House commenced Sept. 1804 and opened 21 June 1805'. The former building was then reduced in size by partial conversion to cottages leaving the central section only intact; by 1968 it had fallen into serious disrepair but it has since (1976–9) been rehabilitated and restored to its original size.

The chapel, which stands on the E side of a narrow alley behind no. 63 Church Street, 200 yards N of the Abbey Church, is a timber-framed building with a tiled roof. The structure originated about 1500 as a hall-house of three bays, the hall in the centre rising through two storeys with a smoke louvre in the roof and two-storied bays to N and south. The framing of the front wall, until recently covered by plaster, has been exposed and many missing or decayed timbers replaced; it comprises a series of large panels with an intermediate rail and two lower braces only between the cill and principal posts. The rear wall is very plain with evidence only for one upper window in the middle bay, of three lights, now blocked. The windows in the

South-West Elevation

Section aa

Front of Gallery

N

The Old Baptist Chapel
TEWKESBURY
Gloucestershire

(Before restoration)

Scale of Feet

5   0   5   10   15   20

Exterior before restoration.

Exterior after restoration.

Interior before restoration.

W front date from the 18th century or later, the central part being lit by two pairs of tall windows separated by the intermediate posts of the framing but cutting through the horizontal rail; a doorway was inserted below the southernmost window *c*.1805 but the window has now been restored to its former length; two upper windows and one below at each end have modern frames; the two remaining doorways which gave access to the early 19th-century cottages appear to have served as the entrances to the chapel.

The interior (reduced to 18ft square in 1805, now 18ft by 48ft) has an 18th-century segmental plaster barrel-vault above a moulded cornice which extends from the S end of the range to an upper vestry at the north. An earlier plaster ceiling just above this vault remains at collar level. Above a stairwell in the NE corner is a smaller vaulted ceiling. The pulpit is centrally placed against the W wall. Galleries around three sides have plain panelled fronts and moulded cornices, supported on the E by two turned oak posts with moulded capitals and tall bases; a further post incorporated in the staircase of the S cottage has been re-used. Walls were built in 1805 on the line of the N and S galleries but the fronts remained intact and the lower parts of the walls received a dado of two tiers of panelling. An upper vestry at the N end has a shuttered opening towards the chapel on the S side with late 18th-century boxing but renewed shutters.

Fittings – *Baptistery*: centrally in floor with steps at N end, brick-lined with narrow channel to W perhaps for filling and drain in SW corner, late 18th-century. *Chandeliers*: two, one of brass with six branches, 18th-century, one with turned wood body and formerly four metal arms, perhaps later. *Communion Tables*: two, one of oak with turned legs and altered top, late 17th-century, one with shaped legs, from Seventh-day Baptist chapel at Natton (see Ashchurch (2) above), 18th-century. *Inscriptions and Scratchings*: on wall plaster outside vestry next to NE stair, 'Hy Jenks', 'R. Yarnal 1795', 'I.E. 1797', and a figure of a cockerel. *Monuments*: in burial-ground N of chapel, many headstones and some table-tombs, (1) John Cowell, 1680 or 1681; (2) Mary wife of John Cowell, 16[?79]; (3) Margaret Millington 'twice widdow', 1684; (4) Richard Field, 1689; (5) Anne Attkinson, 1706; (6) William Steven, 1706; (7) Isaac Straford, 1792, 'many years deacon', Ann his widow, 1793, and Joseph their son, 1813. (Ivimey also records a monument to Eleazer Herring V.D.M., 1694, Mary his wife, 1690, Eleazer their son, 1695, and Anna Flower their daughter, 1760.) *Pulpit*: polygonal with panelled front and moulded dentil cornice, panelled back-board with shaped top and short cornice, *c*.1760, stairs later. *Seating*: before 1976 some fragments of fixed pews remained in the E gallery and open-backed benches, wall benches and stools below; stepped seating formerly in N gallery may be inferred from height of remaining *hat pegs* above vestry shutters.

Arnold (1960) 103–4, figs 9, 15: Ivimey II (1814) 167–8: VCH *Gloucestershire* VIII (1968) 163: White I (1971) 18 sqq.

(146) BAPTIST, Barton Street (SO 894326). Brick with hipped slate roof, built 1804–5 to supersede the foregoing ('plan by Rev. William Bradby') and schoolrooms added behind in 1839–40. It stands concealed behind other buildings on the S side of the street; the plain front has a brick dentil eaves cornice and two round-arched windows formerly with doorways below but altered in the mid 19th century and a central doorway inserted re-using an original canopy on shaped brackets. The sides have round-arched windows divided into two tiers in 1852. Gallery around three sides supported by cast-iron columns of six-foil section. Pulpit and seating renewed *c*.1892.

Benefaction Table: painted 1845 on wall plaster of rear room, recording items from 1749. *Monument*: in chapel, Rev. Daniel Trotman, 1850, 40 years pastor, and Rev. Jesse Hewett, 1843, six years co-pastor.

Ivimey IV (1830) 481–2.

(147) CONGREGATIONAL, Barton Street (SO 895327). Three licences for Congregational preachers were issued in 1672 including one for William Davison, ejected rector of Notgrove, Glos., but the society which had developed by the early 18th century, perhaps from these origins, was Presbyterian and continued to be so described until the later years of that century. By 1819, when Henry Welsford became minister of what was by then an Independent church, the cause is said to have been 'in a very low state', but during his ministry the meeting-house was much altered and enlarged, possibly amounting to a rebuilding in 1828 which is approximately the date of the present building. The chapel, of brick with a hipped slate roof, has a broad front of three bays with a low parapet, round-arched upper windows with shorter windows below and a central porch.

VCH *Gloucestershire* VIII (1968) 164.

(148) Former FRIENDS, Barton Street (SO 89423263). The Friends' *burial-ground* in St Mary's Lane, 50 yards NE of the Old

Baptist Chapel (SO 890325), now a public garden, is reputed to have been in use from 1660. A conveyance of 1670 of 'three messuages in St Mary Street, Tewkesbury, with a parcel of ground where a barn formerly stood, now made use of by Quakers for a burial-ground on the West side, and the tenements of William Clarke the Younger on the East side' is followed by a further deed of 1677 in which the three messuages are described as in use as a Quaker meeting-place. Two timber-framed cottages on the E side of the burial-ground, although no longer exhibiting evidence of former use, may thus be identified as a former meeting-house.

The erection of a new meeting-house in Tewkesbury was proposed in 1794, but the site in Barton Street was not acquired until 1804; the building appears to have been erected in 1805 although the trust deed was not completed until 1810. By 1850 the new premises had proved to be too large and were let, meetings being held in private rooms. In 1861 the meeting-house, which had been in use as 'The Music Hall' or 'Philharmonic Hall', was sold to the nearby Baptist church which used it until 1880 for Sunday-school purposes. It was converted for its present use as a public hall (The 'George Watson Memorial Hall') in 1909. This has brick walls and a hipped slate roof. The front wall, partly obscured by later work, has a brick cornice and parapet and one blind semicircular arched recess with rubbed brick voussoirs. The interior was entirely altered in 1962.

THORNBURY   *Avon*

(149) BAPTIST, Gillingstool (ST 640900). Three-bay front with pointed-arched windows. Built 1828.

(150) CONGREGATIONAL, Chapel Street (ST 637899). Generally similar to the last but with round-arched windows. Dated 1826. (URC)

(151) Former FRIENDS, St John Street (ST 638901). A meeting was established by the late 17th century and a new meeting-house was erected in 1702. In 1792 Friends proposed to demolish two ruined tenements adjacent to this and to use the site for a new building; this was accomplished in 1794 and the present structure was registered in 1795. The meeting-house was closed in 1847 on union with Olveston and in the next year consideration was given to its lease for use as a school; it was sold in 1934.

The former meeting-house, now used as a builders' warehouse, has rubble walls rendered to N and E, and a hipped roof

covered at the back with pantiles. The plan is rectangular (38ft by 24ft) with a narrower wing projecting to the south. The E front, which includes the side wall of the wing, has a wide segmental-arched doorway with a pedimented canopy supported by shaped brackets, now fallen away, and a small tablet above dated 1794; each side of the entrance is a tall segmental-arched sash window. Two windows of a similar size occupy each of the N and S walls, those to the S having segmental heads with brick arches. The S end of the wing is gabled and has a projecting chimney-breast.

The principal meeting-room (25½ft by 24ft) at the W end has a boarded dado and segmental vaulted ceiling; an entrance passage to the E has a small room to the N and a women's meeting-room to the S with hinged shutters (now removed) on its W side. (Demolition of S wing proposed 1983)

THRUPP

(152) WESLEYAN, Brimscombe (SO 868022). Gabled front of three bays with two tiers of round-arched windows. Opened 1804.

ULEY

(153) Former BAPTIST (ST 790983). 'Betheseda Chapel' built 1821, coursed stone walls with polygonal front and large tablet

above entrance. Gallery around five sides with fielded panelled front supported by iron columns. (Closed before 1971, now in secular use)

(154) Former CONGREGATIONAL (ST 784981). 'Union Chapel', built in 1790 for a church which claimed to have been formed in 1735. The pedimented front having a cusped lunette in the typanum with a shield-shaped tablet bearing the date of erection, closely resembles Dursley Tabernacle (70) of 1808 for which it may have formed a model.

The interior (40½ft by 30½ft) has a plaster ceiling with a coved cornice. A gallery around three sides is supported by iron columns of quatrefoil section; the gallery front, pulpit and ceiling were renewed in the late 19th century.

Fittings – *Chair*: in back room, panelled back with pointed-arched top and turned supports to arms, late 18th-century.

Monuments: in chapel (1) Thomas Tilley, 1814, 'of this Village, Artist, whose abilities promis'd An high degree of future fame . . . ', also John Tilley, 1842, Martha his wife, 1824, Sarah their daughter, 1821, and Isaac Ford her husband, 1858; (2) Daniel Neale, 1844, yeoman, and Sarah his widow, 1849, signed Jackson, Uley; (3) Timothy Jackson, 1803; (4) Nathaniel Lloyd, 1808, and Elizabeth his wife, 1807; (5) James Harris, 1801, and Mary his widow, 1814, signed Cooke, Gloster. *Plate*: includes two cups of 1792 given by James Uley Harris. (Closed *c*.1972 and now in secular use)

WESTON SUBEDGE

(155) Former WESLEYAN (SP 125409), now 'Vale Cottage'. Built 1836.

WHITESHILL

(156) CONGREGATIONAL, Ruscombe (SO 838075). Stone and slate with two tiers of round-arched windows, built 1856 to replace Zion Chapel of 1825 which was then used for school purposes. New school built 1934 incorporates date-tablet from former chapel. (URC)
    CYB (1935) 257.

WICK AND ABSON   *Avon*

(157) CONGREGATIONAL, Wick (ST 707726). Three-bay gabled front inscribed 'WICK TABERNACLE 1837'. (URC)

WICKWAR   *Avon*

(158) CONGREGATIONAL, High Street (ST 724884). Gabled front with ball finials, later tablet 'BUILT 1817 RESTORED 1919'. The original back gallery and pulpit with reeded angle-panels survive from the 1919 refitting. *Monuments*: in chapel (1) Moses son of Moses and Elizabeth Amos, 1834; (2) Rev. William Summers, 1825, first pastor, B . . . his wife, 1818, and Mrs Ann Dartnall, their daughter, 1821.

WINCHCOMBE

(159) Former BAPTIST, High Street (SP 025283). Behind a 17th-century range on the N side of the street and approached through

a passage with semicircular arch at the S end inscribed 'BAPTIST CHAPEL JAN 1 1811'; this last marks the date of formation of the church and the approximate year of erection of the chapel. The church appears to have united with Congregationalists about 1878 when Union Chapel was built although a separate Baptist congregation may have resulted from the merger and continued to meet here; the chapel is now used for social purposes.

The walls are of coursed stone with an ashlar front and hipped slate roof. The S front has a low plinth and a platband at mid height. A central doorway from which a small gabled porch has been removed replaced a window in the late 19th century, the two original entrances being in the adjacent bays; three upper windows with stone lintels have had their frames replaced by sheet glass. Two tall side windows have timber lintels. There is a gallery at the S end.

WINSTONE

(160) BAPTIST (SO 959095). Rubble with half-hipped roof; built *c*.1822, two-storied N wing added. *Monument*: Richard Shipway, 1844, and Sarah his wife, 1844, slab with brass plate.

WINTERBOURNE   *Avon*

(161) FRENCHAY CHAPEL (ST 640776), at the N side of Frenchay Common was built in the early 18th century. Although the deeds of the site commence in 1692 there is little trace of Presbyterian activity until early in the following century when in 1704 a house at Frenchay was registered for their use. A further

certificate was issued in January 1724 for a house in Winterbourne and in June of that year the house of Robert Abbotts in the tything of Hambrooke was similarly recorded. Accounts of expenditure do not commence until 1755 but the provision of a bell in 1752, cited when it was recast in 1836, could imply the completion of the tower somewhat later than the body of the chapel. A major refitting was carried out in 1800–1 at a reported cost of £335 5s. 8½d. which probably included alterations to the windows and gallery; further repairs continued throughout the 19th century. The chapel was closed by the then Unitarian congregation *c*.1964 but reopened in 1980 after protracted repairs.

The chapel has rubble walls and a hipped tiled roof in two parallel ranges. The front is symmetrical about a central porch, which rises to form a small tower of four stages divided by stepped string-courses and having a moulded stone cornice and pyramidal roof surmounted by a ball finial and weather-vane. In the lower stage the outer S doorway has a flat-arched head and is flanked by pilasters, now much decayed; on the W side a smaller doorway has been blocked. The second stage has a circular window to the S below the segmental-arched head of an earlier window of different form; on the E side a segmental-arched upper doorway has been blocked. At the top of the third stage, on the S side is a small stone block cut out with a circular architrave and keystones, the centre is painted to resemble a circular window but splayed reveals internally appear to allow for an opening in this position. The top stage has large segmental-arched belfry openings on three faces and a narrow slit to the north.

The E and W walls of the chapel originally had pairs of

(161) WINTERBOURNE. Frenchay Chapel from SW. *Photograph* © *R. Winstone.*

South Elevation

West Elevation

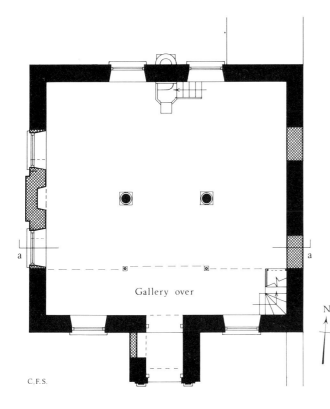

Gallery over

N

C.F.S.

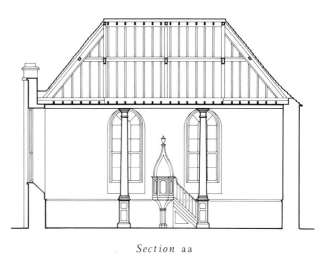

Section a a

Frenchay Chapel, WINTERBOURNE
Gloucestershire

Scale of Feet

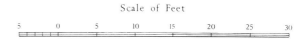

5   0   5   10   15   20   25   30

(162) WINTERBOURNE. Friends' meeting-house. W wall.

windows at gallery level and below; in the alterations of 1800–1 the E windows were blocked and those to the W replaced by windows matching those in the front wall; a chimney-breast was also added against the W wall and a parapet replaced eaves around three sides of the building. The N wall has two round-arched windows flanking the pulpit.

The interior (29½ft by 30¾ft) has two timber columns with Tuscan capitals and high bases supporting the principal E–W beam of the roof. An early 19th-century gallery along the S side with panelled front on two columns may supersede end galleries which were allowed for in the fenestration. *Pulpit* against the N wall, contemporary with the refitting, flared base, panelled front with applied mouldings and a tall ogee back-board with urn finial. Many fragments of box-pews and other seating mostly of *c.*1800 which remained in 1971 have not been reinstated. Other fittings include – *Bell*: one, formerly in tower, given 1752 by R. Allbright, recast 1836 (stolen *c.*1970). *Monuments*: in burial-ground, near porch (1) small slab inscribed 'A S 1701'; against N wall, (2) Robert Bruce 1838, merchant of Bristol, Mary (Dye) his wife, 1809, Robert their son, 1874, and Isabella his widow, 1880, gradrooned urn on pedestal against pointed-arched backing. Also several table-tombs, small headstones and other fragments laid flat, early 18th-century and later. *Weather-vane*: on tower, representation of a comet (possibly Halley's, which appeared 1759), 18th century. *Plate*: includes a two-handled cup of 1728 given by E. Garlick, 1755.

Evans (1897) 89–90: Murch (1835) 48–52: *UHST* VI (1935–8) 260–1.

(162) FRIENDS, Frenchay (ST 641779). Meetings were held in the vicinity of Frenchay from *c.*1654 and a meeting-house believed to have been built *c.*1670–3 was registered in 1689. This was replaced in 1808–9 by the present building which has a stable wing at the front above which a women's meeting-house was built in 1815.

The meeting-house has walls of rubble and hipped roofs covered with patent tiles. The E front which had two arched windows is now largely concealed by two wings with a narrow gap between, the N wing being a cottage of two stories and the larger S wing having to the lower level a stable with passage to the left and the women's meeting-house above with two round-arched windows with external shutters facing the road. The W wall also has two arched windows above a covered walk and near the N end a small two-storied wing with two rooms intended for the use of travelling ministers.

The principal meeting-house has a through-passage at the S end giving access to the burial-ground at the rear and a central entrance; the room has a coved plaster ceiling, a S gallery closed above and below with vertically sliding shutters, and a stand at the N end with an arched window behind. *Book*: Bible, in two volumes, translated by Anthony Purver, (1702–77, schoolmaster at Frenchay and Clerk of the Meeting), published 1764.

Vintner, D., *The Friends Meeting House, Frenchay* (1970).

(163) CONGREGATIONAL, Whiteshill (ST 645793). Half-hipped roof behind swept parapet; three-bay front with round-arched windows, tablet dated 1816. 'Whiteshill Day School' behind.

(164) WESLEYAN, Watleys End (ST 658811). 'Salem Chapel', opened 1790, has rubble walls and a slate roof. The broad W front has three round-arched windows with altered glazing and a late 19th-century gabled porch; two similar windows in rear wall, one upper window at N end. Two-storied Sunday-school adjacent to south. Interior (41¼ft by 25¾ft) has an early 19th-century N gallery, otherwise refitted in late 19th century. *Monuments* in burial-ground to W date from *c*.1830.

(165) FREE METHODIST, Watleys End (ST 659 814). The chapel, no longer in regular use by 1974, has walls of coursed rubble with Bath stone dressings and a patent-tiled roof. The gabled front has a tablet inscribed 'Ebenezer Chapel 1868' above a later porch.

WOODCHESTER

(166) BAPTIST, Atcombe Road (SO 839020). Gabled front with tall finial and round-arched windows; dated 1825.

WOODMANCOTE

(167) COUNTESS OF HUNTINGDON'S CONNEXION, Stockwell Lane (SO 974273). Gabled S front dated 1854 with stone bellcote containing one bell and shield-of-arms of the Countess of Huntingdon below.

WOTTON-UNDER-EDGE

(168) OLD TOWN MEETING-HOUSE (ST 758934). A Presbyterian society which originated in the late 17th century registered the present building as 'newly erected' in January 1702. The society (now URC) became Congregational by the 19th century and between 1898–1904 drastically remodelled the building. The walls (externally 48ft by 26¼ft) are of rubble and the roof is covered with stone slates; the windows are entirely altered but a bracketed eaves cornice at the side next to the road may be of the 18th century and a round-arched window over the end entrance could also antedate the alterations.

(169) THE TABERNACLE (ST 756936) was built in 1852 on the site of the original Tabernacle erected for a congregation formed *c*.1771 by the Rev. Rowland Hill and which eventually became Congregational. The building (sold in 1973 for secular use) was designed by Henry Masters of Bristol in a 13th-century Gothic style. The S front is flanked by small staircase towers intended to rise to open octagonal turrets, only one of which was completed.

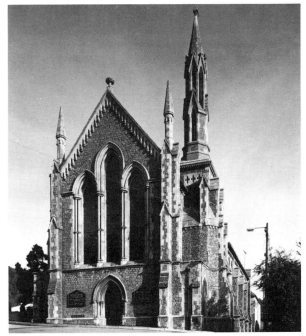

The interior has a gallery around three sides, a pulpit at the N end and a staircase behind leading up from the adjacent Tabernacle House.

Tabernacle House, of brick with stone dressings and a hipped roof, dates from the late 18th century. The N front of three bays has Venetian windows at each end of the two principal floors and a round-arched window above the doorway.

Fittings in chapel – *Bell*: loose in vestibule, small, with painted inscription recording its provenance in the former Tabernacle. *Inscription*: on tablet in vestibule 'ERECTED A.D. 1852 ON THE SITE OF THE TABERNACLE BUILT BY REVd. ROWLAND HILL A.D. 1771 HENRY MASTERS ARCHITECT'. *Monuments*: (1) Rev. Rowland Hill A.M., 1833, founder and minister, with bust in low relief; (2) Rev. Theophilus Jones, 1833.

CYB (1853) 259–60.

(170) Former WESLEYAN, Haw Street (ST 755933). Brick with round-arched windows, gabled front with tablet 'EBENEZER CHAPEL 1805'. Superseded 1896.

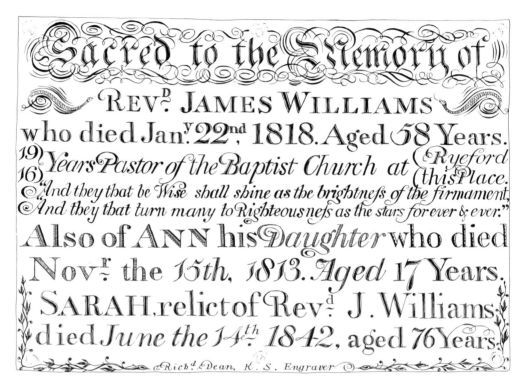

(87) KING'S STANLEY. Baptist chapel, Middleyard. Brass inscription plate.